O9-BTI-667

Make Them Choose You

The Executive Selection Process— Replacing Mystery with Strategy

JAMES D. KOHLMANN

Prentice Hall, Englewood Cliffs, New Jersey 07632

Library of Congress Cataloging-in-Publication Data

KOHLMANN, JAMES D.
    Make them choose you.
    1. Employment interviewing.   I. Title.
HF5549.5.I6K58   1988   650.1'4   87–17435
ISBN 0–13–547878–2

Editorial/production supervision
    and interior design: *Claudia Citarella*
Cover design: *Ben Santora*
Manufacturing buyer: *Paula Benevento*

The publisher offers discounts on this book when ordered
in bulk quantities. For more information, write:
    Special Sales/College Marketing
    Prentice-Hall, Inc.
    College Technical and Reference Division
    Englewood Cliffs, New Jersey 07632

 ©1988 by Prentice Hall
A Division of Simon & Schuster
Englewood Cliffs, New Jersey 07632

All rights reserved. No part of this book may be reproduced,
in any form or by any means,
without permission in writing from the publisher.

Printed in the United States of America

10 9 8 7 6 5 4 3 2

ISBN   0-13-547878-2   025

PRENTICE-HALL INTERNATIONAL (UK) LIMITED, *London*
PRENTICE-HALL OF AUSTRALIA PTY. LIMITED, *Sydney*
PRENTICE-HALL CANADA INC., Toronto
PRENTICE-HALL HISPANOAMERICANA, S.A., *Mexico*
PRENTICE-HALL OF INDIA PRIVATE LIMITED, *New Delhi*
PRENTICE-HALL OF JAPAN, INC., *Tokyo*
SIMON & SCHUSTER ASIA PTE. LTD., *Singapore*
EDITORA PRENTICE-HALL DO BRASIL, LTDA., *Rio de Janeiro*

HF
5549.5
I6
K58
1988

ROCKHURST COLLEGE LIBRARY

20.96

2/90

9780135478783

130060

To my lovely wife
GLORIA
whose constant support, understanding, and insight
contributed immeasurably to this work.

Contents

Preface:
You Really Need
to Know This First!

An important development in recent years has been the emergence of increasing numbers of women taking on professional and executive roles previously held almost entirely by men. This trend has progressed to the point that the companies of which I am aware rarely make any distinction as to preferred gender when seeking to fill key positions.

Although this may be good news for women and the economy as a whole, some challenges arise when writing a book such as this. As most people know, standard English grammatical usage assumes that male pronouns include the female gender as well when they are found in a general context. In light of the above, that practice can leave some women feeling excluded. Since this work involves in-depth discussion of serious interactions between people, it uses lots of pronouns, without which the repetition of names and titles would be endless. Furthermore, the repeated use of "he or she, him or her," and so on would quickly become tiresome to any reader regardless of gender.

To maintain readability without slighting those in the growing ranks of women professionals, I have attempted to bring some balance into the matter of pronouns. In several of the chapters, the majority of personal references are to female candidates and managers so that women reading this book will feel properly included. Since the English language has no gender inclusive pronoun, I'm sure male readers will recognize the fairness of this approach in light of present-day realities.

I warn you of this so that when you proceed from one chapter to the next you won't wonder whether somehow the players in question have changed. I trust each person attempting to identify with the situations presented here will have no trouble continuing to do so from chapter to chapter. This is admittedly a compromise, but the best and fairest I could make on behalf of both men and women seeking to advance their careers.

Introduction

Whether you spend a fair amount of time in boardrooms as a corporate officer or simply aspire to be in such a position one day, you must have the ability to perform well in a job interview. With bankruptcies, mergers, takeovers, and leveraged buyouts disrupting the careers of so many white-collar workers at all levels of management, the fact is that few people feel secure anymore. For these and many other reasons, company loyalties continue to decline, the bond between employer and employee is ever more tenuous, and professional people thus find themselves trying to build careers in an environment of increasing mobility and upheaval. In such a world, knowing how to interview for a job and be impressive is not a luxury—it's a survival skill.

According to the experts, a young person just graduated from college will probably change jobs seven or eight times during the course of his or her professional career. Making those changes will almost inevitably involve both detailed scrutiny of one's qualifications and fierce competition for a limited number of openings. Since there exists no absolute measure of which person is, in fact, the most qualified for any opening, the job offer is usually extended to the candidate who *appears* most qualified.

Senior executives who have been around the job interview track a few times in their careers should not assume this doesn't apply to them. Actually, it is in the boardroom where the emotional, visceral deciding factors most come into play. When the time comes for selection, assuming all candidates are strangers to the management, those intimations, hints, and signals of competence—those appearances—will likely be decisive.

This is a book about how to improve your "appearance." It begins where many other books get vague—at the door to the employer's office. It assumes that a competently prepared résumé has done its job and afforded you a meeting with someone who believes you might be an asset to his or her company. Everything in your job search—the self-appraisal, the research, the writing, the ad-answering, and phone calling—the whole task of marketing yourself—has led you to this door. Or perhaps somebody just called you out of the blue one day and you decided to see whether it really was opportunity knocking. Either way, there's a person beyond that door who may be able to offer you the chance of a lifetime. What are you going to say?

Sadly, most people don't know what to say or how to say it. There are so many ways to blow a job interview that it's not surprising they get one rejection letter after another, even though it seemed at the outset that they were well qualified. The average executive doesn't learn from these mistakes because he doesn't know he made them—the employer doesn't make known his negative reactions and certainly doesn't counsel the hapless candidate in the company's letter of regret, so the same mistakes in interviewing hound the executive throughout his career.

As with everything else, minor fumbles have less effect than major blunders but the wrong step at the wrong time always hurts. I've learned that executives from the major, wealthy, quality employers that everyone wants to join exhibit one common characteristic. They are superb performers when being interviewed—brisk, clear and concise in their presentation, factual without being boring and totally in command of themselves. They are a joy to interview and we recruiters take special pains to see that our best clients are informed of their talents, because we know they will be impressed with our selection of such clearly superior individuals for their inspection. Not only is an impressed client a happy client, but the candidate benefits from exposure to the very best companies under the most agreeable circumstances. All this evolves from the ability to interview well.

I have first-hand knowledge of the myriad mistakes people make in interviews because my clients tell me about them. Early in my career, I just threw up my hands when a seemingly well qualified applicant of mine did something foolish and was consequently removed from further consideration. Later, armed with data from literally hundreds of interviews, I began to study the patterns that explained why one candidate did well and another, even better qualified person, did poorly. I developed some very specific assumptions about the selection process and how any job candidate could use them to develop his or her interviewing skills.

In time, these studies produced an outline of strategies and tactics that I felt would benefit candidates who were about to be interviewed. I gave a formal presentation of these ideas to every candidate presented for interview to my clients. Over the years, professionals at every level, from people just a few years out of college to senior executives, received this presentation as a condition of introduction. The results were astounding. Detailed follow-up questioning of both clients and candidates revealed the true benefit of such consultation. The candidates related how much more relaxed and confident they were, knowing what to do and how to do it. The clients were likewise impressed and, although they knew nothing about the counseling, more frequently wanted second interviews and more frequently made offers. Today, I will not submit a candidate without preparing him or her for the encounter.

What you are about to read is designed to approximate a long counseling session. The contents consist mainly of field-tested techniques for dealing with the psychological pressures of such important meetings so as to achieve desired results. It delves into the hidden buildup of internal motivating factors that lead an employer to a hiring decision and how they can be used to the candidate's advantage. Furthermore, it gives detailed coverage on how to negotiate for the best possible compensation as well as tips for evaluating the potential size and likelihood of discretionary incentives.

It is the constant modification and refinement of this interview preparation program, plus the continuous monitoring of those strategies and techniques that have proved particularly useful, that form the basis for this book. If you find these ideas useful, there is no reason why you cannot read the whole thing again before every interview. You never know what may strike you in a new way that meets your immediate need.

Incidentally, I'd be very interested in your accounts of how these strategies may have been helpful, or any other comments you care to make. Please contact me in care of the publisher.

1
Appearance versus Reality

Being able to present oneself well in a job interview is similar, I suppose, to our modern conception of what the Old West must have been like: Most cowboys did not have to use their six guns every day, but on those occasions when it was necessary there was no substitute for ability gained through practice. Unfortunately most people do not spend a great deal of time, if any at all, practicing their job interview skills; therefore, when the need for them arises, their lack becomes evident to the person who should discern it least if the outcome is to be successful—the employer's representative. Even those rare people who give some thought to the techniques involved gain very little by practicing with their friends or before a television camera. There are simply too may intricacies in the relationship between the interviewer and interviewee for such activity to approximate a real-life situation.

This is really a shame, because the net effect is that the system tends to reward those who are essentially good actors and to punish those who, whatever their genuine talents, are not able to present them with the necessary flair. So it is not uncommon to find in American business articulate, extroverted people of limited capability in positions of major importance while, on the other end of the spectrum, there are too many stories of truly talented people who have spent their entire working lives unchallenged and unrewarded because they were unable to get that "big break."

The situation is, however, not hopeless. While one cannot practice job interviewing skills, it is nevertheless possible to understand the process so that it becomes predictable and therefore much less frightening. It is this method which offers the greatest hope to the average job seeker—not hours spent in front of a video camera or rehearsing what one will say, but learning the psychology of the entire job interview ritual so that one feels comfortable in the environment as much as possible. It is to the ritualistic nature of the matter that we should now turn.

The first thing to understand is that the job interview is not a pleasant conversation between two people attempting to arrive at a common goal. It is, rather, like those peculiar Arctic birds you may remember from watching the wonderful nature films Walt Disney produced so many years ago; you know, the birds that would develop a love interest in each other by hopping up and down on one foot, circling each other in a clockwise direction, and bobbing their heads about in some sort of coded pattern that at least made sense to them. If one of the birds was too dense to know which foot to hop with or which direction to circle, the other bird wrote him off as hopeless and went in search of some other, more "with it" bird who knew how to dance. The same thing is true in the business world: You either know how to "dance" or you'll find yourself left out when the really great opportunities become available.

I'm trying to say that a job interview is more like a mating ritual than anything else. It is more precise in its forms and protocols than any other ritual in business, with the possible exception of the firing of a senior executive by a board of directors.

With this understanding, when the interviewer smiles, shakes hands, and suggests that you sit down and relax, you should know that he is merely engaged in the first move of the ritual. If you are wise, you will not relax even for a moment, any more than you would if you had just gone on stage in your debut as the lead in a Broadway musical. Likewise in the job interview; from the moment you see this man's or woman's face, you are on stage.

The interesting thing about the job interview ritual is that so little of it is physical, or even verbal. To a certain extent it consists of the nature of the give and take between the two parties, but more than that, its real substance lies in the underlying thought processes in the mind of each person that produce the dynamics of the encounter. This does not diminish in any way the ritualistic nature of what is happening—it just makes the right moves harder to figure out. Some people do it right almost by instinct (like those birds we talked about). You can learn to do it right by design.

You may think, because this ritual is so hard to discern, that I am making the whole thing up; sort of a modern version of the emperor's new clothes. Let me tell you, though, that in all the years I've been a professional recruiter, from cutting my teeth on $10,000-a-year trainee jobs ten years ago to my current work on executive assignments paying ten times that much, the pattern which I describe is remarkably consistent. With rare exceptions the situations in which a job is ultimately offered involve a strict adherence to the ritual. I know this because part of my assignment is to question closely both job candidate and employer representative to determine how the interview went. Having done this literally thousands of times, for a vast array of different positions and salary levels, I can tell you unequivocally that when this hidden pattern is followed correctly, the natural result is that the company gets properly in the hiring mood and makes an offer, if, of course, the applicant is not manifestly unqualified. Indeed, on those few occasions when I know for a fact that the ritual was not followed, it invariably became known to me later that there had been some prior contact between the hiring manager and person under consideration.

But we are dealing with a different situation; one in which the company representative, or hiring manager, and the job applicant, or interviewee, are total strangers to one another and have no perceived common interests or acquaintances. Under these circumstances I reiterate that the job interview ritual will be firmly adhered to, at least in the mind of the employer.

To make matters more obscure, the employer representative (whom we shall interchangeably call the *hiring manager* or *interviewer*) is as consciously unaware of the nature of this ritual as the person being interviewed. Employers act as though they were literally following a script, but were you to suggest such a thing to them, they would likely respond, "Of course not!" and tell you about their individual style and the special things they look for in a candidate. Nevertheless, the mental pattern can be found regardless of style or manner of questioning. It is there whether the interviewer knows it or not.

You can observe something similar by visiting an art gallery. One person may be a student of art and can tell you the history of any given artist, the philosophy of the school in which he was taught, and why he tended to use a lot of red in his "blue period." Another man may simply respond, "I don't know much about art, but I know what I like." In fact, if they both find themselves bidding for the same canvas, they will each bid with equal diligence. The first one knows he wants it through a process of reasoning and evaluation, while the second one just "likes" it. Watching these two go at it, you would be hard pressed to tell who was the art scholar and who was buying on intuition. Both are, after all, waving green money in the air.

Therefore, you must know this: Employers hire job candidates on intuition. They may talk all they like about their interview systems and their special techniques for eliciting the truth from reluctant interviewees, but the real decision to choose one and reject the other will be made on intuition. It is all well and good for the job applicant to present a carefully prepared résumé and fill out the application form neatly and completely, but these things represent perhaps 10 percent of the ingredients upon which a decision will be made. Whether the candidate is seeking a trainee job or a position as corporate executive, it is my unshakable belief that some 90 percent of that decision to hire is made on viscera or "gut feel." That's the same as intuition.

When you think about it, what else has the hiring manager really got to go on? You can't present 10 years of experience on two sheets of paper, no matter how good a writer you are. Fill ten pages, and I guarantee you they will never be read. Résumés like that invariably go to the bottom of the stack while the executive makes the mental note, "I'll wade through that after lunch (a week from some Thursday)." Similarly, even if you had some interviewer's attention for five straight hours, you could not really tell him everything you did and how you did it over a period of several years. Psychological testing has proved itself less than totally reliable in predicting success on a new job, and even intelligence batteries are not sure-fire. Finally, reference checks can be a two-edged sword because, as litigation against former employers becomes more successful every year, the hiring manager may hear neutral or even positive things about a real bad apple because the former employer doesn't want any trouble.

Thus you perceive another great truth: Job offers go to the applicants who *appear* most qualified, since it is nigh impossible to determine from the limited data available who is *really* most qualified. Even though appearances can be deceiving, the job interview and the perceptions gained by it are still the most heavily used tools to determine who gets the offer.

This means that over the course of from one to four meetings, each lasting anywhere between 45 minutes and several hours, the company representative will generate 90 percent of the information upon which to make a decision. How well I remember those frustrating occasions when, as a young recruiter, a company would give me a contingency assignment based upon very strict job qualifications—the candidate must have so many years of experience in such and such industry, with this degree and that professional certification, and so on. Believing these to be the genuine criteria upon which I would earn my fee, I diligently sought such people. Older and wiser competitors, knowing the nature of this game better than I, would seek out candidates whom they believed would appeal intuitively to the hiring manager in question. Sure enough, after weeks of work and having presented several candidates, knowing that I was in competition with others, I would call the company to discover that my candidates had lost out. I would carefully ask the hiring manager, "What was the selected person's background?" I'd be dumbfounded to learn that there was no certification, and he came from a different industry, and he had fewer years of experience than those I had presented. So I would then ask, sweetly of course (one must never ruffle the feathers of a hiring manager), "Whatever made you hire him, then?" The inevitable reply, delivered in the blandest possible tone: "Well, I liked him." It is from such experiences, repeated over time, that one, it is to be hoped, learns a few lessons.

Now it does not matter in the least to the employer that he doesn't understand or appreciate the irony of this situation. After all, he has no interest in the process itself. The hiring manager enters the room in total command of the proceedings. It is his company and his job to offer. He's there to get information, form an impression of the applicant, make a decision accordingly, and get on about his work. He does not think in terms of whether the interview "went well" or not; he's only interested in discovering whether he "likes" the applicant. To analyze the internal processes by which he arrives at a decision is, for him, a waste of precious time.

You, on the other hand, have every motive in the world to understand the process. If you can get inside the head of this person whom you will be talking with, you can determine, in advance, what responses from you will generate positive feedback, what questions will be received enthusiastically, and, in general, how to handle your part in the ritual. Without such information, the job applicant in an interview is like an airplane pilot navigating by dead reckoning; he knows he's over a city in Kansas, but nothing more than that. This is an unenviable position in which to find oneself if there's a genuine need to land the airplane. Likewise, every job applicant knows that he or she must get the employer representative to "like" him or her, but the question remains how to do it. This is particularly difficult when a talented company interviewer will give off few signals as to whether the interview is going well or not.

Having established the importance of understanding that the job interview is a precise ritual and that those who recognize this and act accordingly will be rewarded while those who do not will be disappointed, let's delve into the matter in more detail.

2
First Impressions

Before we examine what actually happens during the interview itself, some mundane but very important topics need to be discussed. Since success in the interview is determined by a wide variety of intangible elements, no single aspect of the process can be overlooked without courting disaster. It is not enough to do most things right, because there's no such thing as "almost hired" in one's record of success. You are either offered the job or you are not. In this context, where sufficient inattention to any detail may be enough to turn the company away from you, everything is important.

The first thing is, of course, appearance. As some philosopher once said, "You never get a second chance to make a good first impression." The image which registers in the mind of the hiring manager as he or she walks forward to shake your hand will be one of the most long-lasting determinants of the final decision. It may not be fair (certainly rarely relevant to the content of the job), or even particularly intelligent, but the fact remains that appearance is a major element in whether or not one is considered a viable job candidate. To make the situation worse, it is not always even a matter of grooming or the tailoring of your clothes. It is abundantly clear from analyzing human nature that handsome men and attractive women are more sought after in society than those less fortunate in the looks department. This unfortunately carries over into the hiring process, the theory perhaps being that good-looking employees give the company a better "image." While you cannot do a great deal to change the looks you were born with, you can gild what you have in such a way as to maximize the power of your presence.

Properly groomed hair, freshly shined shoes, and well manicured fingernails are sufficiently obvious that we won't dwell on these essentials. That's not to say they can be overlooked, though, because these things say something about your habits and personal hygiene. And herein hangs a tale that is very relevant to the entire interview process.

Interviewers extrapolate much more information about your character and conduct from this initial meeting than they would from any other kind of similar business discussion. Hiring managers assume, quite rightly, that a person being interviewed for a professional position is on his or her very best behavior. This being the case, any aberration or omissions of appropriate conduct during the interview will be taken as red flags by the hiring manager. He will reason that if this is the best you can do when you are watching every move, what in heaven's name will you be like six months from the date of hire, when you are greatly more relaxed than during the interview. For example, the man who twiddles his thumbs in an interview may be perceived as someone so nervous that in an unguarded moment he may just begin jumping up and down on his desk. The woman who speaks in a hushed monotone may be perceived as extraordinarily dull. These extrapolations are not really fair, but they are part of the reality of the interview ritual, and you may as well accept it.

It therefore follows that a person who does not attend to the obvious details of grooming for such an important event as a job interview will invariably be perceived as one of poor breeding, and if he dresses improperly as well, the interviewer will add the comment "lacks taste." Lest you think I am dwelling too much on this, let me say that I have watched more than one important job offer slip away from an otherwise qualified candidate because he did not pay attention to the fundamentals of personal appearance. As we shall see later, the task of hiring a key individual has its risks for the hiring manager, and he will thus be highly disinclined to take any more chances than necessary. An unkempt job applicant has a powerful negative impression to overcome, no matter how talented he is.

Clothing should generally be conservative unless you are seeking a job in a recognized "glamour" industry, such as film making or advertising, or unless you know something about the personality of the hiring manager and the evidence indicates that he will be receptive to more modern dress. Your clothing should call attention to you, not to itself. In the absence of information to the contrary, one can hardly go wrong with a navy suit, white shirt, and solid tie. Women should dress in something equally staid. For those who wish a fuller discussion of clothing in the business environment, I can hardly do better than recommend *Dress for Success* by John T. Molloy. In paperback it will cost you a few dollars and tell you more than you ever wanted to know about how to dress for almost any occasion, including a job interview.

One other point involves the matter of cologne or perfume. This is not a date, and the feelings that cosmetic manufacturers seek to arouse do not have a legitimate business application. Neither do you want the interviewer looking at you through eyes watering from the fumes you've brought into the room with you. In this context, the most attractive aroma is *clean*, with a judicious application of anti-perspirant (to take the worry out of being within six feet of each other). Aside from this, you want nothing more than a bit of after shave lotion, or subdued cologne for women. Some breath spray wouldn't hurt, either, particularly if the interview is scheduled after a meal.

Assuming that you are now in the company representative's reception area, dressed in a manner appropriate for meeting the President of the United States, the next thing you will confront is normally some kind of employment application. This must be filled out neatly and with great care, particular attention being paid to several areas.

In the place where the application asks for your reason for leaving or desiring to leave your most recent position, write "*Will explain in interview.*" Do not elaborate. In the space which calls for your desired or expected salary, write "*open.*" Do not elaborate. Also write "OPEN" in any spaces which ask whether you will travel, relocate, work part time, and so on. *Open* is a very useful word in these circumstances, because it does not commit you to anything while at the same time it suggests that you are not an inflexible type. Indeed, the purpose of this technique is to ensure that you make no value judgments whatever on the application. This way, the company representative will not have the opportunity to form some negative opinion of you based upon the value judgments he perceives while reading the application before even seeing your face.

Contrast this approach with the impression created by an application which reads, "Salary desired: *Minimum 25 percent increase*; Relocate?: *no*; Travel?: *no*; Work overtime?: *no*; Reason for leaving last position: *Personal conflict with boss.*" One might reasonably conclude that the employer's representative will read this litany of negatives and form a less than complimentary mental image of the writer before even shaking hands. By looking at this extreme example (which I have seen in real life, by the way), you can see the wisdom of saving your ammunition for the actual encounter.

One more word about the application is in order. Many professionals, having spent considerable hours and money creating a crisp, thorough résumé, respond to the application with a good bit of annoyance. They demonstrate this by filling the application out in an offhand manner or scrawling across the front of it, "*See résumé.*" This is an outstanding way to start off on the wrong foot with the company representative. You created the résumé to get in the door.

The résumé has served its purpose, and you will not endear yourself to anyone by implying that the application form is stupid, unnecessary, or both. Many intelligent interviewers scribble furiously on the application, to which they constantly refer during the course of the meeting. They want something to scribble on, and they want the application to be filled out neatly and carefully so that the comments they make on the form relate properly to the information provided by the applicant. This is not an unreasonable request, and applicants who imply that they are too important to go along with the program do themselves no favor by making an issue of it.

As we shall see later, most interviewers who know what they are doing have a very definite mental game plan which they intend to follow during the course of the discussion. Most of them have done this more than once and, as creatures of habit like all of us, they develop a pattern to aid in the speed and thoroughness of their work. There is particular information which they look for in a particular order. Since everyone does a résumé a little differently, it becomes very difficult for the interviewer to follow his comfortable pattern if he has to search the résumé each time he wishes to bring up a new topic. The application provides him with a means to methodically cover all the areas of interest in the easiest way. Wise job applicants, therefore, recognize his legitimate requirement and fill out the application without any undue fuss. After all, at this point you want something from the interviewer. He doesn't even know yet if you have anything to offer in return.

You are now prepared to enter "the room." You will be meeting with a person who has a problem and has come to believe that you can somehow help solve it. On the conscious level, he is looking for "just the facts, Ma'am." Subconsciously, he is seeking something much deeper. Your assignment is to give him the facts and, without his knowing you have done it deliberately, give him the other as well.

3

Shooting at the Target— Not Your Foot

Many job applicants have trouble in interviews because they don't know why they're there in the first place. Naturally the surface reason is to get a job, to make the company representative like him or her, and to appear the best candidate available for the position. But these obvious goals are of no help at all when it comes to developing tactics. What specifically do you do to get the hiring manager to like you? What exactly is involved in creating the appearance of being the most qualified candidate? It is not simply a question of discussing your work experience and smiling at the right time. There is a great deal more to it than that.

Some job applicants believe that the interview represents an opportunity for both parties to evaluate each other. The company examines the job qualifications of the applicant, and the applicant evaluates the desirability of the job. Nothing could be further from the truth. This serious misconception of the interview ritual is responsible for more rejection by companies of genuinely qualified candidates than any other single factor in the process. A wise job applicant, therefore, knows that his or her initial assignment is exclusively to get the company interested. Any activity in the interview which is not geared to this result is time wasted and, at worst, can be extremely damaging. Any attempt to make the company representative justify the value of the job at issue or the quality of the firm he works for is, at this stage of the process, an invitation to disaster. To put it another way, the ritual demands that the company gets the ball first. Another rule is that the company remains on offense until it willingly gives control of the matter to the candidate by making a job offer. Only then is the candidate in a position to "control" anything. Any attempt to wrest control of the meeting from the employer representative prior to that event will produce highly negative results.

To see why this is so, let us consider for the moment the situation and motivation of the hiring manager. This person, as we said before, has a problem. The interview is his attempt to determine whether your presence in the company will help solve that problem. The problem may be large or small; the fact is that he must solve it, and he is inquiring whether you can be any use in helping him do it. Were this not the case, the meeting would have no purpose, and the hiring manager would be simply a manager going about his everyday tasks.

Remember that the problem is not that one of his subordinates has quit or been fired and that an opening exists. That's just the outward indication that there's a problem. The real problem is the work piling up on the former employee's desk; the overtime that must be paid to make up for his or her absence; the extra hours that the hiring manager must himself put in to keep the department above water while a replacement is sought; the ideas not being generated because the former employee happened to be particularly brilliant. *That's* the problem.

Supervisors, department heads, vice-presidents and other members of management, almost without exception, dislike interviewing. They regard it as an intrusion upon an already busy schedule, something which consumes valuable time, and something which in all cases except one produces no results. It's a necessary task which is nonetheless keeping them from the pressing work that is their real responsibility. These people do not like interviewing and, to further complicate matters, most of them are not very good at it. They are, for the most part, not trained in the techniques of eliciting sensitive information and therefore approach the whole business with a certain amount of reluctance. Add to this the political reality that if such a person makes a serious mistake by hiring the wrong key individual and the company suffers for it, the one who did the hiring may incur permanent career damage as a result.

You should begin to see how the emotional tone of the whole meeting must simply be considered delicate indeed. He does not really want this meeting, but he has a problem which cannot be solved without it. He is poorly equipped to handle the situation; nevertheless he must do so and must conduct the meeting in such a way that a substantial amount of hard information is gained from a total stranger. Further, a certain portion of that information may well be uncomplimentary, and the interviewee will take some pains to see that it is not revealed. The hiring manager must get it anyway, because it will in all likelihood be the stuff on which his final decision must be based. Moreover, if he doesn't make the right decision, his own career may be seriously jeopardized.

If you view the hiring manager's situation in this light, you will fully realize the application and importance of all that is said later on. And you will begin to fathom how the feelings necessary to making an optimum hiring decision become a growing reality that leads to action. If the hiring manager's psychological makeup is indeed this way, you must do certain things to ensure that an already unpleasant prospect is not made a more unpleasant experience.

First, you must concentrate on creating in his mind the idea that you are there wanting to help, to serve, and to make his problem go away. You must literally make him feel that by having your presence in his company, his sleep will be sounder, his food will taste better, and his life will in all respects be more lovely because the problem will now be yours and not his directly—and he can count on you to handle things properly. You will take the burden from his stooped shoulders and place it upon your own, and he will never see it again.

This is not exactly realistic, but then we are dealing with the person's hopes and fond wishes, not cold reality. Almost all people indulge in a bit of fantasy when faced with intangible problems or possibilities. Many cold-eyed professionals are the same people who buy time-share condominiums in Barbados and sight-unseen land in some retirement paradise. As a particularly sharp salesman for one of Florida's most notorious retail land sales companies told me once, "We never sold land—we sold dreams."

Therefore, it is imperative that you concentrate strictly on demonstrating to whatever extent possible how you can solve the problem at hand. You should see by now that, in the initial stages of the interview, any effort by you to evaluate things such as salary, benefits, hours, and the like will simply muddy the water. You run the very distinct risk of saying something that will alienate the person you are trying to impress and all for nothing. The plain fact is that until you have a job offer from the company, you have nothing to evaluate.

Your immediate strategic objective is thus made clear—get a job offer. In this phase of the process you are not negotiating; you are selling. You do not care whether the offer is good or bad, lucrative or penurious, with convenient hours or work every weekend—you care only that the company has focused upon you to the exclusion of all others who have applied for the job. Once the company has properly focused, once they say, "We want you," then you may go on to the next part of the ritual and begin to think about whether you want them.

This approach admittedly involves risks, the greatest being that you may invest a great deal of time and effort pursuing a job only to discover that it really isn't for you. There is perhaps nothing more upsetting than to invest several hours of time in a variety of interviews with the same firm and then be told that their maximum offer to you is several thousand dollars less than the minimum you will take. The temptation to find out up front whether the job is worth going after is almost irresistible, but you must resist it anyway. Unless you are the most adroit, diplomatic semantician in your city, another Henry Kissinger in the making, any effort on your part to address employee-need questions will cause the company to react in a negative way.

Instead of impressing the hiring manager, you will put him on the spot; instead of demonstrating your willingness to work, you will be manifesting an aspect of, let's face it, greed. Instead of discussing the employer's problem with which he is most, even exclusively, concerned, you will turn the discussion to your problems and needs, about which frankly he could not care less. If the job is worth going after at all, you may as well do it right. Invest the time, play the game, participate in the ritual, and then see whether the fish you have finally caught is worth mounting on the wall or whether you should just throw it back in the water and try again. To do otherwise is to seriously reduce your ratio of offers to interviews. Again let me say that this is not a theory—this advice is given after evaluating thousands of interviews from not only the candidate's perspective but also that of the hiring manager. The conclusion that premature discussion of employee-need questions produces irreparable harm is inescapable.

So many candidates are appalled at the idea of subordinating their desires to those of the employer that I have developed a special illustration to drive the point home. Indeed, it seems the more senior the executive, the more distaste there is for approaching the interview this way and these are precisely the people who need this instruction the most. Egotism is never particularly attractive, but in an initial job interview it can be the kiss of death. The job candidate must behave in many respects like a salesperson, and the good folks in that field know they must invariably defer at all times to the wishes, whims, and agendas of prospective buyers. So must it be with the job applicant who hopes to get anywhere.

Think of one of those old-time mercury column thermometers that you may remember from a grade-school textbook. Imagine that the thermometer is placed in a liquid and that the effectiveness of your interview presentation will determine how high the column of mercury goes. Marked on the glass tube of the thermometer are two lines, one somewhere near the top labeled "hire," and one a good way further down that says "forget it." Assuming the level of mercury stands somewhere between these two the moment you shake hands with your interviewer, here is what should happen.

By playing to the interviewer, by seeking to solve his problem, by being agreeable, by dismissing your own desires as not worth mentioning at this point, by creating the appearance of competence, by conducting yourself professionally, you raise the temperature of our hypothetical liquid and consequently the level of mercury rises as the conversation progresses. If things go properly the column will pass the "hire" line and the employer will begin thinking in terms of an offer. But you can't stop there because you obviously don't know where the line is and, even if it's been passed, the interviewer doubtless won't say, "Okay, you've said enough, I think you're good, you're hired."

The selling continues until the offer actually materializes and this may occur days or even weeks later. Thus, you must continue to be agreeable and professional and concerned about the company's problems and so on, driving the column of mercury clear through the top of the glass if you can do it. The more excited the hiring manager becomes about bringing you aboard, the less attractive taking time with other candidates will be and the more quickly he is likely to move in your direction.

I might note that this illustration is relevant after the offer has been made also. You'll see why when you come to Chapter 14, "Now that They Are Yours," in which we discuss what you do when you have an offer and you're wondering whether or not to accept. Suffice to say that the thermometer is still in the liquid even at that stage but instead of the conversation producing rising temperature it will result in a cooling off. At that point you will be asking the questions, tough ones I hope. Your needs and desires will be the main focus and, understandably, the hiring manager will be less inclined to treat these subjects with the same warmth that was evident in the matter of solving the company's problems. Every time you bring up something you want it will likely be coming out of the company's hide, of which this person is a representative. You may perhaps see how the level of mercury in our thermometer is about to head south.

You can negotiate all you like, but at some point you may go too far. You may become so demanding, so critical, so skeptical about the firm's financial picture that the employer simply decides that on balance you won't be such an asset after all. In this circumstance the company will think nothing of withdrawing the offer and bidding you a fond farewell. The mercury has at that point dropped to the "forget it" line and you have blown it.

Now, once an offer is made, companies will usually put up with a certain amount of nonsense from selected candidates but there is a limit. Unfortunately, you don't know precisely where that limit is and you'll find it different for each company, each interviewer and each situation right down to the day of the week. The manager who will cheerfully humor you along on the day after the firm has achieved record sales may grunt or snarl about the same issues after learning a major deal has just fallen through. But of course you don't know what kind of day it's been when you go in for these important negotiations.

The bottom line is that since you know neither the location of the "hire" line or the "forget it" line, you have only one possible strategy. By driving the mercury as high as it can possibly go throughout all your interactions with the company until the offer is actually made, you increase the distance between that point and the "forget it" line. This puts you in the best bargaining position and you can negotiate with the firm, confident that, although you may be using up political capital to get your way once the offer is made, you're dickering with them from the most advantageous position you can achieve.

The first candidate upon whom I tried this illustration was mightily thankful for it. This woman, unemployed but with a solid reputation in her field and obviously some money in the bank, planned to entertain a rather prickly interviewer by interrogating him as to whether his company was a worthwhile place to work. In the absence of my counsel, I'm confident she would have done just that and been treated to an early trip home. After seeing this illustration and noting its importance in terms of developing a negotiating position, she changed her tactics and was rewarded with a vice-presidency at that firm and nearly a six figure starting salary. She confided to me later that without the illustration she would not readily have changed her tactics, thereby doubtless losing an outstanding opportunity.

A principal tenet of my argument in these matters is that the company is almost invariably in total control of the process from start to finish. Wise job candidates will recognize this without too much prodding. I make the illustration simply to help you see the light.

In summary, then, you appear initially to the interviewer as a salesman. You are selling a product. Instead of selling beans or hardware or electronic components or insurance, you are selling a [here insert your name]. The nice thing is that you have a great degree of product knowledge (or at least you should have). The unfortunate thing is that most people are simply not salesmen. Because of this, our further discussion will include a short course on how to sell the product, what techniques to use, what to watch out for, and how to answer questions.

4

*The Importance
of Pacing*

There's an old song titled, "Flow Gently, Sweet Afton" which I allude to by saying "flow swiftly, sweet interview." The fact is that an interview can be effectively likened to a river in many significant ways. Before we examine what you should do in an interview, let's discuss what the interviewer is thinking and how you can best make use of that knowledge.

In a previous chapter I noted that most hiring managers do not like interviewing but rather regard it as a necessary evil when there is a job to be filled. To this extent, one can gain immeasurably by making the interview process simple and painless for the interviewer. If an interviewer has to do a lot of work to get the information he or she wants, the meeting will be remembered as more unpleasant than if the information was obtained easily. Simply keep this in mind as we proceed with the balance of our discusssion.

Even though the hiring manager may not enjoy interviewing, she will still regard it as a job to be done and apply her best intellectual effort to seeing it done properly. She will know that certain information must be obtained and will seek to get it in a more or less orderly and logical fashion. In any given interview situation, you may correctly perceive that the interviewer is not very talented at asking questions, but never underestimate her basic intelligence. In most cases, these people don't rise to the position where they are able to offer professional job opportunities to folks like you by being stupid.

The hiring manager will have in her mind some sort of game plan for obtaining the information she needs. This will involve historical data, information on your style of management or working with others, and your personal views about your own motives and attitudes. To get this she will have to ask certain questions and then follow up on each tack until she is satisfied that she has enough information to make a decision. Regardless of any smiles and chit-chat that may accompany the process, you are safest to assume that this person will be going after information in a relentless and thoroughly practical way. By knowing what kind of answers she wants and how she wants them, you can go a long way toward making the interview less of a strain upon you both and earn a lot of what I call "political credits" in the bargain.

If the interview is like a river, it will flow. In other words, it will move logically from one place to another in a smooth and continuous fashion. It may begin with a discussion of your education, moving on to your first job, from there to the reasons that you selected your next job, and so forth. It may, on the other hand, begin with your present employment, going backward in time and finishing up with your education, or even with your childhood. In whichever order, or in whatever way, the interviewer chooses to obtain information, it is a flowing process where the talk about one section of your life or work dissolves into talk about the next.

Your first tactical goal, therefore, is to make the "river" flow as smoothly and swiftly as possible. A smoothly flowing interview is one in which the interviewer is not distracted by employee-need digressions, in which there are no power plays over who is in control of the meeting, in which there is no extraneous matter discussed such as the latest fashions or the antics of one's children (unless the interviewer instigates it)—in short, an interview where the hiring manager can readily get to work and concentrate on the subject at hand.

The swiftly flowing interview is the one in which the hiring manager has the luxury of asking only a few questions and still getting all the information she needs. This means that you must invariably give her more information than she asks for but not so much that it becomes distracting. It's quite a balancing act, but done properly pays enormous dividends in the formation of our warm fuzzy orange ball, about which more later.

There are a variety of ways to mess this up, and most job candidates seem to go to one extreme or the other. Some people believe that the less said in an interview the better, perhaps on the theory that if you say little there is less likelihood of saying something stupid. This may be a good tactic for your first date, but it is completely inappropriate for a job interview. In this circumstance the river is more like a glacier, and the hiring manager, in order to obtain the data she needs, must ask numerous questions and be rewarded with only little bits of information. You can see how this will rapidly become frustrating, irritating to her, and ultimately destructive to your purpose. Monosyllabic answers of the "yes," "no," "Fort Worth," "1965" variety are to be avoided at all costs. Remember: You are selling a product, not responding to an inquisition from the FBI. You must not only deliver the information but must do so in such a way that the interviewer is glad to have it and doesn't feel she invested too much time and effort in getting it.

The other extreme is equally damaging, if not more so. This

may be likened to attempting to dig tributaries to our hypothetical river rather than being content to let it flow along within its original banks. There are those individuals who believe that when the interviewer asks a question, she really wants their entire life history at that exact moment. When she asks about their current employer, they think she wants the company's story from its founding in 1930 to the present; when she asks about their job function, that she wants them to quote verbatim a three-page job description; and when she asks about high school, that she wants a rendition of their most impressive solo as lead singer in the glee club. Actually, of course, she really doesn't want any of that.

Those who find themselves busily trenching away in this fashion put the interviewer in a very awkward spot. The trouble is that she wants certain answers in a brisk, no-nonsense way, and she isn't getting them. This makes the interviewer choose between two mildly unpleasant alternatives: She can either continue to listen to that which is both unproductive and time wasting, or she can cut the applicant off in mid-sentence and bring him back to the mainstream of the conversation. However the manager handles it, the long-winded one sitting in front of her is definitely not doing his job-seeking cause any good.

The typical response will be to listen for a while and hope that the applicant will soon tire of this and decide to return to the important subject at hand without any prodding. Most people, including hiring managers, dislike conflict and will naturally be a little reluctant to tell someone forcefully that what he or she is saying is irrelevant. This involves a certain amount of emotional tension which, although slight, is enough to keep many managers listening and nodding their heads while at the same time thinking how nice it would be if this applicant would begin to discuss something of substance. The real danger is that there is no direct correlation between a person's willingness to put up with this and her degree of irritation at having to do so. There are plenty of Walter Mitty types in this world, who are one thing on the outside and another on the inside, and some of them find themselves in the role of hiring manager from time to time. It is possible for a hiring manager to nod and smile while the interviewee goes through a long discussion of some obscure topic, but inwardly she may be seething that this witless so-and-so is taking up her valuable time with verbal garbage. If such is the case, the applicant's chances of getting a job offer approach the odds of hitting the jackpot at Las Vegas.

The job candidate is in far better shape if the person interviewing him is the acerbic type who won't stand for this kind of thing for very long. The manager who is abrupt and not much of a diplomat will quickly sense when useless chatter is taking place, interrupt, and swiftly bring the conversation back on track. The candidate may be a little unnerved at this, but for the hiring manager there is almost no emotional tension, so it may not so severely affect the candidate's overall chances. Nevertheless, if an interviewee is interrupted more than twice for being excessively long-winded, she should take it as a cue to change her style quickly. Once this type of hiring manager concludes that such verbosity is an unchangeable part of the candidate's persona, the possibility of a job offer is likely to vanish forever.

While on this subject, we should note that it is not only my rather facetious example of the glee club that can be the culprit in these situations. You may be discussing completely relevant aspects of your most recent position or the situation surrounding your desire to move to another city and the like. Keep in mind, though, that what you want to tell the interviewer is not important (except in certain situations discussed later). The only important thing at this stage is that the interviewer gets the information she wants and gets it in a straightforward and relatively painless fashion. In this regard, you must constantly be taking the interviewer's temperature to see the attitude in which she asks questions, how many questions she has to ask before seeming satisfied on a particular matter, and the degree of satisfaction she seems to express when getting the answers. The rule of thumb is that the fewer questions the interviewer must ask to obtain full satisfaction on a particular topic, the better you are doing. Nevertheless, don't get into so much detail that you begin to irritate her by adding information she doesn't want at that time.

To illustrate, let's suppose that the interviewer is asking about your most recent position. She may say something like,

"I see that you are now with General Motors."

It's very possible that she may leave it at that to see what your response will be. This is a completely open-ended statement and can elicit responses that range from "yes" to a thorough description of everything you have ever done since the day you first walked in the door at General Motors 20 years ago. Actually, neither of these replies is appropriate. The first indicates to her that she will have to ask many, many questions to get the information she needs. The second kind of answer will either produce numerous interruptions to bring the applicant back to the "mainstream" or an increasingly disinterested listener whose mind will continually wander to the things that are not being accomplished because she must sit in front of this chatterbox.

Although no generalization can cover every situation, a few definite things can be said about how to handle this aspect of the interview. First, most knowledgeable interviewers are consistent in their desire to know several things: (1) the month and year in which you began and ended your various jobs, (2) the way in which you found the job, (3) your title, (4) the name and/or title of the person you report to, (5) the number of people you supervise (if any) and (6) something about the company itself unless it is a household word such as General Motors.

Therefore, your opening line if the interviewer's comment is, "I see that you are with XYZ Corporation" might go something like this:

"Yes, I joined XYZ Corporation in June of 1981. I responded to an advertisement they ran in the local paper and was chosen from a field of about 75 candidates. XYZ Corporation is involved in several lines of manufacturing, and their gross sales volume is about $70 million annually. I was hired as Customer Service Manager reporting to the Director of Sales, and I now supervise five people."

This is a brilliant answer! It gives a lot of hard information quickly, in such a way that the interviewer has some sort of feel for your company and your place in it. There's a little sales pitch that you were chosen from a large group of applicants, yet it leaves the interviewer free to pursue a variety of lines of questioning. She may wish to know more about the firm, or may wish to know more about your job duties, or she may go directly into a discussion of your management style. Whichever way she goes, you are doing an important thing by answering in this way—making the interview easy for her. Although I may seem to be belaboring this subject, you'll find as we go along that the value of creating this kind of atmosphere with the interviewer cannot be overestimated. The warm fuzzy orange ball is beginning to form on schedule.

5

Selling by Asking Questions Yourself

There will typically come a place in the meeting at which the interviewer will say something like, "I suppose you have some questions about our company?"

This is usually the point at which the untutored candidate launches into his or her own agenda and expresses an interest in salary, length of lunch hour, vacation policy, and benefits. Such an approach is all well and good if you want to gather information about a company for which you don't plan to work. I have been told by hiring managers and personnel directors at the highest level that whenever a candidate begins discussing these issues at this point in the interview, it is an immediate and almost invariable turnoff. Such conduct will sour the hiring manager's attitude toward you in nothing flat. The reason is that the interview ritual requires that he offer to answer some questions. Nevertheless, he is still interested in solving his problem and a discussion of salary and benefits, while it may certainly interest you, moves him no closer to achieving his goal. As I said before, your proper tactic at this point is to appear in the role of a servant, a serf, a slave whose whole existence will be wrapped up in solving this person's problem. This is an artifice, of course, as is most everything else in the interview process, but it must be done. The hiring manager is not stupid—he knows you are interested in salary and benefits. He knows that this subject will have to be addressed if you are an attractive candidate and he wants to have you on his team. But while he is in the process of making up his mind whether he really does want you, this employee-need discussion is a total distraction to him. It serves no useful purpose and it is immensely irritating to think, "This individual sitting across from me is interested in joining my company so that he can take my money, avail himself of my benefits, and take a nice vacation every year at my expense." If you want to blow your chances completely, there is no better way to do it.

Having struck that nail once more, let me go to the positive side of your opportunity to ask questions. It affords you the most outstanding opening to sell yourself that will occur, perhaps in the entire interview process. If handled properly, you can make the employer think that you are brilliant, dedicated, and hardworking without ever saying a single thing about yourself. It is indeed sad that so many candidates take this golden moment and use it to throw away their chances rather than solidify them.

Stated briefly, you are going to want to ask three different kinds of questions, all of which will speak directly to the employer's need while at the same time painting you in the most favorable possible light. The first thing to ask about is the work. Not the position—the work, the task, the challenge. You need to ask detailed, linked, strictly job-oriented questions about everything you can think of that relates to the work.

It is truly amazing how many job applicants will be satisfied with a ten-second description of a job and then go on to asking the really important questions—like salary, benefits, and so on. Ironic is the fact that, were the hiring manager to suddenly declare, "You're hired, you sit there, the restroom is down the hall, start now," they would have a million questions, all of which would have to be answered to some extent before they could begin to function effectively. The key is to ask those questions in the interview before you are hired.

This pays enormous dividends. First, it indicates to the hiring manager that you are work-oriented, not position- or job-title-oriented. He has offered to answer questions and you dive immediately into the tasks necessary to solve his problem. Second, if your questions are intelligent and follow a logical thought pattern, he will conclude that you are reasonably bright. How many times have I been in discussion with hiring managers after an interview and heard them say about a properly prepared candidate, "He asked very good questions." Third, if you do this effectively, the hiring manager will, at the end of the interview, recognize that he has given you a great deal of information that he would otherwise have to give you at orientation after you are hired. His task of training is therefore somewhat reduced and, if he hires you, he will be getting someone who already has a pretty firm grasp of the basics involved in getting the job done. So—you're hardworking, you're bright, and the manager will think to himself, "We actually got something accomplished that I won't have to do over again." Not a bad set of feelings for the prospective employer to have as the door closes behind you.

Asking intelligent questions along this line is not all that difficult. Simply place yourself mentally in the position of a new employee approaching this person as a boss and wanting to understand what goes on in the department so that you can be effective. Next, consider the essence of the problem which has been outlined to you so far in the interview. If it has not been articulated, your first question should be something like, "What is the most pressing problem this department has?" Once you hear the problem, you can then ask, "When did you first notice it?" or "What steps have been tried to correct it?" or "Who has been responsible for that area in the past?" You can then continue with, "Tell me about the procedures that must be followed in handling responsibility for solving the problem at hand." Perhaps, "What analysis has been done so far to isolate the cause of the problem?"

Once, using this or a similar line of questioning, you have some grasp of what is keeping this person awake at night, go on to other aspects of the job. "How does this department relate to the company as a whole?", "What sort of improvements or modernizations are contemplated to make the work of this department more efficient?", "What do you see as the outstanding characteristics of your most successful subordinates?" There is a vast number of job-related questions which you can legitimately ask, each of which will give you further insight into the manager, his department, and the challenge at hand.

This is one area where I counsel job candidates not to be timid. My advice is typically to push the manager almost to the point of irritation in your relentless drumbeat of job-related, task-related, policy-related, procedure-related questions. You want to use this chance to soak up as much information about the job itself as possible. In all the thousands of interviews that I have evaluated with hiring managers, never once have I heard one of them say, "I don't want that fellow, he's too interested in the work!" It's not surprising. After all, the job in question is the whole point of the discussion from the hiring manager's perspective. He wants someone who will get as deeply into the problem as he is. He wants someone who will become as involved in seeking solutions as he is. He wants someone who will shoulder the burden. Obviously, the individual who asks relevant, probing questions will appear far more willing to accept that responsibility than someone who asks two or three questions and then goes on to other things.

It should be noted that the job interview is unlike any other business meeting because, in it, the parties are focused on each other and not some problem, project, or transaction. The only similar thing is, of course, a firing, a termination, or, as the euphemism is known these days, a de-hiring. In both such cases, the focus is exclusively on the other person, and this probably accounts for a good portion of the emotional delicacy that we've been talking about.

There is a way, however, in which you can score even more points through your job-related questioning and that is by getting the hiring manager so deeply involved in a discussion of the challenges at hand that he turns his focus from you as a candidate to you as a potential collaborator in solving whatever problems exist. Handled properly, your questions should put you on "his side of the desk," as it were, and you both turn your attention to a third thing, which is the task itself. If you can, by dint of creative, intelligent questioning, produce such a collegial atmosphere that the hiring manager begins to discuss his departmental problems with you as though you were already aboard and expected to work on them, that sequence of give and take will make an indelible impression on the manager, and it will definitely be recalled when decision time comes. I don't hesitate to say that if you can create five or ten minutes of this kind of interpersonal harmony, you will have achieved the pinnacle of success in terms of making a lasting, positive contribution to your cause.

I would also point out that you should not interrupt your effort along these lines to comment about your own prowess or experience in doing similar things. This is not the time for the hard sell. This is the time for selling without selling—the time for demonstrating an aspect of your competence rather than telling about it. There are times when a direct selling approach is used, but it's not a sales pitch. There is only one sales pitch in this meeting, and that occurs at the very end.

You should try to spend not less than fifteen minutes in direct question and answer interchange about the job duties as outlined above. Then, you will have to judge from the warmth of the interviewer's manner or, perhaps, the abruptness of his answers, whether you are reaching the point where he thinks the topic has been discussed enough. In many ways, the most long-lasting impression you want to leave with this person is the depth of information you have obtained about the job as a result of the interview.

You must use the bulk of your questioning time to discuss the job and its duties and responsibilities as outlined above. If, however, you've developed a clear understanding of what is required and the hiring manager has not indicated a desire to either retake control of the proceedings or wind things up, you may continue to the second type of question, which has to do with the company itself.

Here you are not only attempting to elicit information,

perhaps to compare with that gleaned in a personnel-type interview (discussed later), but also to give the hiring manager the idea that you want to work for *his* company, not just any old company. Most people are, or should be, proud of the place they work; if they're not, it's reasonable to wonder what they're doing there. Since part of your task in the interview is to get the interviewer to feel good about you, there is nothing wrong with asking questions designed to elicit answers that will make him feel good about himself and his company.

You can ask about history, unusual successes, particularly popular products, rare innovations brought forth from his department, anything of a positive nature. Obviously, you don't ask questions which will put the hiring manager on the spot or elicit negative feelings—that comes after the offer has been extended as we shall see.

If, after five minutes of this, your hiring manager is still in an affable mood and willing to humor you further, you can ask about the company's future, most specifically your future within the company if you remain with them for a significant length of time. Not only will this gain you some insight as to how he or she perceives the job and its possibilities, but also you create in the manager's mind the idea that you do indeed intend to remain with the firm and make a long-term contribution. In an age when lots of people change jobs every year for one reason or another, this is no small impression to make. Here again, you are selling without selling. It is creating a feeling by asking a question. It offers the double advantage of providing information to you as well as generating goodwill with the interviewer.

Once you have covered these three topics—job responsibility, the company itself, and future prospects—you stop. There are really no other legitimate questions for you to ask at this stage that don't use up more political capital than the responses they produce are worth. If your hiring manager lets you go to these lengths to obtain information, you can be reasonably sure you've made a pretty good impression; otherwise, you'd have gotten signals to stop. If you're permitted to go all the way through the three phases, you will learn a great deal and make significant points for yourself.

Keep in mind, though, that you must be constantly on the alert for signs of irritation from the hiring manager. That's why the sequence is so important; you get the critical information first and, if time and circumstances permit, then go after the other. You can push the interviewer to the point of irritation only because you're discussing things that relate only superficially to your own needs; otherwise you'd never get away with it. Don't push beyond that point, however. If you do, all the gains you've made may well be lost if the most deeply etched memory of the meeting becomes exasperation at having had to answer so many questions.

This is a delicate arena in which to operate, but playing the game right at this stage will pay enormous dividends. You will see later how it all comes together to make you appear the best qualified person for the job.

6
The Deadliest Question

It should be rather clear by now that a great deal of what you are doing to make the interview process work for you is anticipating what the interviewer will most likely want to hear. There is nothing unsportsmanlike about this because, after all, you have an objective, too. This is a vastly preferable situation than the one which occurs in most job interviews, namely, that the interviewer has a definite program and objective while the applicant is simply being manipulated to conform to that program. No rational interviewer should object if the person to whom she is speaking is bright enough to have an agenda of his or her own and clever enough to implement it. This leads us to one of the most critical yet hard to discern aspects of the entire process which we might call, "the deadliest question."

As we have seen, most interviews consist of a reasonably straightforward question-and-answer format. The wise candidate will respond narratively, giving a significant amount of detail with each answer but not going so far as to bore her listener or to give information that may be interesting but which the interviewer, for her own reasons, finds irrelevant. There are a variety of different styles used by interviewers, but for now we are still discussing general cases. Nevertheless, every job interview will contain one or more situations in which the deadliest question can arise. The job candidate who can anticipate this and parry effectively has made a giant leap toward improving the probability of receiving a job offer. The candidate who does not understand the situation when it arises may very well be excluded from further consideration and simply never know why. Very briefly, the deadliest question is one which is on the interviewer's mind but which, for reasons of her own, she does not articulate and which she then has the temerity to go ahead and answer for herself on your behalf without ever having said a word on the subject. Creating a defense for this purely mental exercise on the part of the interviewer is perhaps the most subtle thing you can do to ensure a successful outcome.

To set the stage for further discussion of this phenomenon, which I'm sure has you extremely puzzled at this point, we must again review the interviewer's mental processes which lead up to the interview itself. Excluding people in the personnel department, whom we shall discuss at a later time, the typical hiring manager who has decided to spend her time interviewing a job applicant has some preconceived ideas about the person whom she will meet. These ideas may come from a résumé, they may come from a quick glance at the job application, or they may come from someone who has recommended the job candidate, either a friend or acquaintance, the personnel office of the company, or a professional third party, such as a recruiter. Unfortunately for the candidate, these preconceived ideas are invariably negative. It is simply a feature of human nature that when we are contemplating a decision we look for reasons to decide against taking a particular course of action. Hiring managers are people too, and therefore they go through the same thing. Since it is almost never true that a job candidate actually fits the ideal description of the person the hiring manager wants, there will always be areas where background, talent, appearance, experience, attitude, or personality could be a little bit better. Most hiring managers are smart enough to know this, and they don't seek perfection. Quite frankly, those that do never hire anyone until circumstances or some higher power in the company suggest that they lower their standards. This being the case, once the hiring manager has decided to interview somebody anyway, those points of nonconformity will stick firmly in her mind and they will be an ever-present aspect of the meeting, though usually a completely silent one.

Remember that interviewers are evaluating all the time throughout the course of the discussion. They know that it will be impossible to cover every aspect of the candidate's history in the one to two hours that they have allotted. They know that, regardless of how well they may conduct the interview, there will be gaps, there will be areas unexplored, and this, in and of itself, adds to the potential uncertainty and risk involved in actually making the hiring decision. No one as yet has found an adequate way out of this dilemma, and it can be safely predicted that hiring managers will be going through these agonies for some decades to come—at least until someone invents a lie detector that is absolutely foolproof and the government allows private business to use it.

With this in mind, let us assume that candidate John Doe is a complete blank to the hiring manager until she reads Mr. Doe's résumé. After that, there is the barest skeleton of the person, which consists of where he spent his time and a bit of what he did. The personnel office may have interviewed Mr. Doe and offered some observations as to appearance, personality, manner of speaking, and other relevant thoughts. At this point the manager still knows almost nothing about the real John Doe. The interview is supposed to supply a sufficiency of additional data from which a sound hiring decision can be made, but the risk factor is still huge. The interview doesn't provide a completely reliable picture, simply because nobody is that good an interviewer. If the hiring manager is sufficiently methodical, sufficiently well informed, and sufficiently clever, she may get to the point of having enough information to form a 50 percent accurate picture of John Doe as he really exists. Since she unfortunately must hire the whole person and not just the part she knows for certain, the balance of the input upon which the hiring decision will be made must consist of hunch, intuition, "reading between the lines," "gut feel"—you name it.

The real difficulty is that for every question an interviewer actually asks, her mind may well be producing a whole host of others on the same topic while she is yet speaking and while she is listening to the candidate's answer to the one she actually asked. There will be such an infinity of different questions, nuances, expansions, and other material that she would like to have if only she had the time to go after it. But the hiring manager is looking at her watch and realizing that the discussion must proceed to other things. Therefore, those questions don't get answered by the candidate. But in many cases, after the interview is over, the hiring manager will reflect upon the meeting and answer the questions herself in an understandable effort to flesh out the data she did get to bring her perception to the point where she can make a decision with some degree of confidence. If this little after-lunch exercise produces a negative impression overall, there is precious little the candidate can do about it. He has, after all, gone his merry way, and the manager is sitting in her office thinking. More than one excellent potential business marriage has been blown sky high by this precise scenario, and the only way in which you can avoid being a similar casualty is to anticipate the unanswered questions and answer them without being asked.

The extent to which this aspect of your campaign looms large will naturally vary. It will be determined principally by the interviewing skill of the person you are meeting, and since you have no idea how good an interviewer this person is, the problem is compounded by total uncertainty. Nevertheless, you cannot afford to ignore it, and your only safe course is to assume that unasked questions will arise in various areas and to be prepared to insert the information you wish to project at the appropriate time. If the interviewer turns out to be very capable and asks you all the questions directly so you can respond in the normal course of events, well and good. If, on the other hand, the interviewer is one of those types who lets you do most of the talking and does very little leading, you will be very glad you prepared responses to questions that never came. Those responses may spell the difference between a second meeting and a very brief letter sent to your home two weeks later.

To take an example, let us suppose that you are a data processing professional with experience on NCR and Honeywell equipment, but the company with whom you are interviewing has IBM equipment. After the pleasantries are over and the interviewer is getting down to business, she may ask, "Have you had any experience with IBM equipment?" since she sees none on your résumé or application. At this time, it might be possible for you to mention that you had worked extensively with IBM equipment for several years in college, which was only three years ago, and thereby defuse a potential problem in the interviewer's mind. But the interviewer might not be quite so bright as that, and she may simply assume that since the IBM experience does not appear on the résumé, it doesn't exist at all. If the question of IBM equipment is a critical one, the impact of your perceived lack of experience may be the deciding factor in passing you by as a viable candidate.

Your approach to dealing with this type of problem involves two facets. The first is a careful assessment of your weaknesses prior to the interview itself. It is very necessary to be completely objective here and you need have no fear of doing so, since you don't plan to reveal whatever weaknesses you discover to anyone else, at least not voluntarily.

Remember though, that when asked a direct question you *must* answer honestly. If you get the job, your boss will know you well enough after three months' employment and if she thinks at any time that you deceived her during the hiring process, your position may well be in serious jeopardy. Second only to theft of company property or money, deception of a hiring manager during the selection process is the fastest way to get fired—with a stone-cold response to requests for references forevermore. Hiring professional people is a tough, risky business, as we have already stated, and companies are just plain unmerciful when they discover they've been lied to about anything of substance by a job applicant whom they subsequently hire. Remember it, and *never* lie.

Returning to your introspection. As with all of us, you are

not an ideal job candidate. There are things about you that are not perfect, and they will have greater or lesser impact upon the hiring decision, depending upon how those things are presented and perceived and their relative importance to the company. Some of these things are not even negatives in and of themselves, but they may impact the hiring manager negatively and must be treated therefore with the same tactics as a short work history or inadequate education. An excellent example of this is the candidate with young children. Hiring managers may make quite a few assumptions about who cares for them, and who tends them when they're sick, but they're not really permitted by either federal law or the conventions of the day to ask questions on these sensitive topics. Here again human nature takes over, and the extreme likelihood is that the hiring manager will be completely silent on the subject and simply make her own evaluation, which may be completely erroneous but which nevertheless represents the data which she will feed into the decision-making process. The candidate faced with this must recognize that it is a potentially negative situation and make plans to bring the subject up himself or herself, set the hiring manager's mind at ease, and thereby defuse a potential bomb. Remember, though, that topics proscribed by EEOC regulations are not the only ones where the questions will simply never be asked. Recall the time pressure factor and the relative levels of interviewing competence possessed by different hiring managers. You must be prepared to deal with all manner of potential negatives by bringing the subjects up yourself and producing a positive statement which will effectively short circuit the hiring manager's tendency to provide her own answer after the fact.

The second part of this tactical approach is that you may sense in the interview itself that the interviewer is worrying some particular aspect of your aptitude or experience; she's honing in on something; there is a problem in her mind. At this point you must attempt to locate that problem without ever saying anything so that you can make sure her mind is at ease on the subject before the interview is over. If you fail to do this, the hiring manager, though she may have asked several questions on the subject, may still be producing her own conjecture as additional facts and again you are deflected from your target by a phenomenon over which you have no control.

A corollary tactic which can be used in the interview itself is that if you have diligently and thoroughly asked job-related ques-

130030

tions, you can discern where the hiring manager's main problem lies. Then, by making a mental comparison between your own experience and aptitude and her immediate need, you can discern for yourself where she might think you are weak and then, again taking the initiative, address that subject with positive statements that will have the effect of reducing her level of concern.

Please note the importance of addressing these issues in a smooth way that flows along with the direction the interview is taking. As mentioned before, an interview is like a river, and it's well to keep that analogy in mind as you seek to carry out the tactics of this chapter. The course of a river may be turned by a strategic placement of barriers or obstacles, or by digging a new channel for it; but one thing you can't do with a river is pick it up and move it 30 feet. Likewise, you cannot jerk the interview around to suit your agenda for making these points we've alluded to. You have to pick your opportunities within the context of the subject matter at hand and gently steer the conversation in such a way that you can make those statements necessary to your own program.

The key is that, even though you may have spent hours contriving your presentation in accordance with the ideas outlined later, not with any intention to deceive but only to be thorough and positive, the interview must appear to produce responses that are spontaneous. Any suggestion to the interviewer that they have indeed been carefully thought out beforehand will have some negative impact. I'm not even sure why this is so, but I've seen it enough over the years to take the phenomenon as given. You should do the same and make the appearance of spontaneity central to your approach.

Your ultimate goal in this aspect of the interview is to insure that, whatever questions the hiring manager may have regarding your abilities, personal situation, or level of experience, you have at least had the opportunity to address these subjects and make the most favorable presentation of yourself possible in these areas. This is not to say that you will be entirely able to satisfy an interviewer on every point. There may indeed be areas where your experience is not everything the person hopes for. But you will at least have created the most positive possible impression and not be a victim of the manager's mental processes going against you without having had the opportunity to input your own information.

This is perhaps a good place to insert material on, not the deadliest question, but the deadliest interview. Each interviewer has his or her own style, and, if called upon to interview frequently, will normally use it in a consistent fashion. There is one situation, however, which is so dreadful that all your talents will have to be employed to present any kind of comprehensive picture from which a decision can intelligently be made. This interview is called "the visit."

Some people, particularly at senior level, are so unfamiliar with what is called for in an interview that they genuinely don't know what to do. If they're high enough in the company, their egos may prevent them from asking for advice, in which case they proceed using their best instincts, which are rarely sufficient for the task at hand. Such people are really at a loss because, as I said before, there is no business proposition to discuss. There is no problem, there is no transaction, no purchase or sale, nothing but the other person. This is an awkward situation for both parties when the one supposed to be in charge doesn't know what to do. Faced with this, your hopelessly incompetent interviewer will usually revert to the style she reserves for cocktail parties. This isn't surprising, since it will be her usual fashion of dealing with strangers where there is no business to talk about, and you will be treated to a pleasant little chat that includes tidbits about the firm, and maybe herself, you'll get to say a bit about yourself and at the end you will both think each other to be wonderful folks, but still total strangers.

The deadly part comes when she is asked to make a decision based upon what was learned at the meeting. Now the horror dawns upon her; you are still as much an unknown as when you walked in the door, and there is hardly any evidence to work with. You may be hired because the interviewer liked you, but it may not be a good thing.

The best illustration I have of this is a recent assignment in which I asked what had gone on before I was given the task of filling a senior-level operations position that had been open almost a year. It turned out that an individual well known to the chief executive by virtue of their attending lots of meetings together was interviewed in just the manner I describe. A delightful meeting took place in the CEO's office, with drinks and delicacies served, and after a few hours the two were feeling quite chummy. A job was offered and accepted, and the new vice-president moved his family from a distant city to the company headquarters with high hopes.

Not one month later the firm learned to its chagrin that this gentleman's strength was in sales and marketing. He knew virtually nothing about operations, and they faced the grim prospect of dismissing him. As a matter of fact, that is exactly what happened, with the company assuaging its guilt at having made such a disastrous mistake by paying him a magnificent severance along with relocation back to his former home. It was an expensive and emotionally trying experience for all concerned, one that could have been avoided had the interview revealed his true abilities rather than the extent to which the two could catch up on old times. With no recruiter or personnel officer to offer objective data on his abilities, the thing was a brewing calamity from the start.

Should it become clear that your interviewer is visiting with you, the following chapters on creating a game plan will pay off more than in any other circumstance. The concept involves work and attention to detail, but its intelligent use will put you miles ahead of the competition in any interview you undertake. In the case of a "visit-type" interview, your game plan may well make the difference between disaster and a golden opportunity.

7

How to Answer
Tough Questions

Up to this point, our emphasis has been on strategy. We have been concerned mainly with broad considerations dealing with the interviewer's motivation and style and the atmosphere that surrounds the entire interview process. This is fine as far as it goes, but the actual interview will invariably consist of a series of questions and answers. To be successful you must have not only some idea of how to say what you want but also what you are going to say.

Many books have been written which purport to suggest brilliant answers for the problems that many of us have, such as a spotty job history or an uncomfortably long total work experience, also indelicately called being too old. It is possible, of course, to offer some clever riposte to questions that deal with these issues, but such answers are unlikely to do much good when the time comes for the company to make an offer. An intelligent hiring manager does not want someone who has had a series of jobs, none of which have lasted longer than six months. There is rarely an adequate answer to explain why you can't remain in someone's employ in a supposedly permanent position long enough to do either of you any good. The only honest advice anyone can possibly give you in a situation like that is to find some kind of legitimate work and stay with that employer for at least three years so that, on your next job hunting venture, you can show the hiring manager some kind of stability. Remember, there is a very definite distinction between making yourself appear to be something you are not and making yourself appear in the best possible light. This book, at least, attempts to do only the latter and, at the risk of repeating myself, I will say again that efforts at the former are almost invariably doomed to failure. People who hire other people for professional-level positions cannot be fooled so easily. They usually become quite annoyed at candidates who try.

The other issue, which we may as well bluntly call the age factor, is simply an unpleasant fact of life. There are numerous laws on the books which declare flatly that it is illegal for companies to discriminate on the basis of age, sex, religion, race, creed, country of national origin, and so forth. The list gets longer with each passing year as more and more groups decide that they are aggrieved parties in these matters and manage to get themselves included. Nevertheless, notwithstanding all the excellent laws, there is a limit to what government in a free society can do in the way of regulation and surveillance. Prejudice is a fact of human existence, and you are going to run into it. If you are someone who has passed his or her fiftieth birthday, there are cases where this alone is going to work against you. There is no brilliant answer that will defuse the issue in the mind of a person who is emotionally biased against older workers. With a manager who is simply seeking competence and examining your record for evidence of it, you won't have to address the subject at all.

Now that you know there is no such thing as a uniquely brilliant answer that will make all your problems go away, we can turn to the positive side of answering questions. Indeed, there are many valuable techniques which can be used to legitimately present your credentials in the best possible light. At the very least, these techniques can help you deal with areas of your background that are not exactly ideal and allow you to discuss them in the least negative light. We shall look at this aspect of the topic first.

Never let a negative stand alone. Did that sink in deeply? Let me repeat. *Never let a negative stand alone.* How's that?

This is a concept which every trainee salesman learns in his or her first few weeks in the field but which, unless you happen to be in sales, you may never have heard. It is a simple concept, easily applied, that has remarkable utility in the interview. Not only this, but failure to use this idea in a tight situation can have a devastating effect upon your chances of receiving an offer simply because human nature dictates that negative information has a greater impact upon us than positive. It may not be the greatest comment on the human condition, but a quick look inside your own heart when someone is telling you things about a third party should be enough to verify its accuracy.

Consider, for a moment, the fact that the interviewer is no dummy. He knows that you are attempting to impress him; he knows that you are selling yourself and your talent with as much ability as you have, and he is therefore likely to regard the positive things you say about yourself with a certain degree of skepticism. He will duly take them down and, if he is a true professional, verify those statements by talking to people for whom and with whom you have worked in the past. Such statements are regarded by the interviewer less as selling points than as evaluation benchmarks, principally useful in directing discussion with any potential references.

On the other hand, any negative comments the interviewer can get you to make about yourself will be viewed as the unvarnished truth, particularly if they are unusually damaging admissions. Since, unlike with the positive statements you make, you have no ulterior motive to offer negative data, the interviewer is quite likely to assume that he has indeed heard the truth when you say, "No, I never did that," or "No, I don't know anything about those types of transactions." When the interviewer hears such things, the information will bore into his brain and remain there, becoming a part of every recollection he has of your meeting with him. At this point you should be thinking that anything which will blunt the effect of this phenomenon is very much worth knowing.

First, though, if you have to say no, you must say *no.* Any attempt to be coy or cute with the interviewer in order to get around the unfortunate fact of your total ignorance in a certain area will almost surely backfire. If you are not clever about it, the interviewer will make his own determination that your observations to the contrary really do mean no. Then instead of one negative, you will be facing two—both the fact that you don't have what he wants and that you tried to hide it. If you are, however, very adroit at dissembling on the subject, a worse thing may occur. You may successfully convince the interviewer that you have knowledge or experience that you don't, in truth, have. Based upon this you may receive and accept a job offer, leaving your existing employer and digging into your new assignment with high hopes. Then, of course, the interviewer as well as everyone else in the company will discover that you indeed don't know anything in some critical area of your supposed expertise. The immediate conclusion which the interviewer will draw, partially to protect himself, of course, is that he was deliberately deceived and had he known the truth, he would never have hired you. The all-too-frequent outcome of something like this is that you wind up fired, with no employer at all, a reference from these new people which is indifferent at best, and some unpleasant explaining which must be done in any future interviews.

So if you must say no, say it. Don't equivocate or dissemble or beat around the bush, because you cannot possibly do your cause any good that way.

There are, however, several things you can do to mitigate the psychological effect of the word "no" when it comes out of your mouth, and this is what those sales trainees are taught. Basically it consists of not allowing the negative statement to hang in the air for any length of time while you and the interviewer stare at each other. Although I have never attempted to reduce this to a mathematical formula, I will say with great certainty that the potential for any negative statement to ultimately kill your chances of a job offer is directly proportional to the length of time the interviewer has to think about it unimpeded by any other verbal input from you. This being the case, the phrase, "No, I never did that" must be followed immediately by something. That something can be anything so long as it is honest and gets the interviewer's attention away from the word "no." For example, you can mention background or experience that is similar, if not identical. And, if you have it, this is perhaps the best defensive technique to use.

Remember that a skilled interviewer is not necessarily looking for a clone of good old Charlie who was with the firm for seven years and has now sought greener pastures elsewhere. The company needs certain skills. Obviously, if the candidate selected comes from the identical industry, serving the same market and dealing with the same kind of distribution structure, the likelihood that those skills are going to be present is much greater than if the similarities don't exist. Nevertheless, the absence of those similarities does not automatically mean that the skills aren't there.

If you do not have similar skills with which to impress the interviewer, the next best thing to follow your negative statement is something about similar educational background. It is possible that you studied problems similar to the ones this company is facing in college or postgraduate courses taken after you entered the work force. Mentioning relevant education signals the hiring manager that your learning curve with respect to his situation may well be shorter than might otherwise be the case, thereby again blunting the impact of the word "no." If you have neither similar experience nor relevant education, your fall-back position is simply a desire to learn this new aspect of your discipline. By making your negative admission with complete frankness and then expressing interest nonetheless with sincerity and the appropriate amount of eagerness, you will be surprised to find that even what appears to be a weak position is remarkably strengthened thereby. Moreover, the impact of the word "no," although clearly stated and duly noted, will not be nearly as severe as if you had allowed the negative to simply hang in the air and make an absolutely indelible impression on the hiring manager.

While honesty is the best, indeed, the only policy to follow in the interview, this does not mean that you are under oath before a grand jury. You don't have to tell the whole truth, baring your soul before this person. You must simply never lie, or give the impression of having lied. Oddly, juries today seem quite forgiving of liars, and one sometimes wonders whatever became of the penalty for perjury. Hiring managers, on the other hand, don't forgive and they don't get mad—they get even. They fire you.

But they don't expect any intelligent candidate to tell everything. After all, they know it's a contest, too. Thus we come to the second great commandment of dealing with negatives—*Never volunteer anything negative about yourself.*

It is amazing how many candidates, in the sincere belief that they are somehow furthering the process, will share personal negative traits or experiences for which the hiring manager has not asked. They just don't know what a devastating effect such revelations can have on the probability of their getting an offer. In many cases, these are observations about former bosses, feelings about certain industries, personality quirks, or features of their work habits that will not be particularly relevant to anyone two months after they have been hired. But in the intensely evaluative atmosphere of the interview, they take on expanded meaning and, because they are offered without prompting, they may leave the interviewer with the idea that they are much more important than they, in fact, are. Remember that the interview is a ritual. Your job is to sell. The interviewer's job is to get information.

It seems to me that a person who volunteers incidental negative information in an interview is like a football team that deliberately moves the ball toward its own goal line. While the opposition is intensely pleased, I have never heard of a football team doing that and achieving anything good by it.

Remember now, we are talking about *incidental* revelations that are not basic to either your performance or the nature of the job at hand. Many times these statements come from candidates in almost a cathartic manner, as though they thought they were in the confessional box rather than at an interview. If you wish to go to confession, do so in church. In the interview, your task is to present yourself as a person of unlimited potential and no problems whatever. The interviewer, of course, will not believe this, because all people have problems. But then when the tables turn, the company wants you badly and you start to hear the same person describe his or her company as a place of unlimited opportunity with no politics, you will—I sincerely hope—realize that this clear nonsense is just another part of the ritual and the hiring manager is simply playing the game, too.

There are, of course, items of negative information that must be offered to the interviewer even if he doesn't seek them out. A person with a severe case of emphysema, for example, had better so inform the interviewer or face the possibility of being offered a position working in an office with 50 people who smoke. A person who has never been a good supervisor of others and knows it would be a fool to cleverly angle for a job offer by not revealing this weakness if the job involves supervising a hundred people. Be sure, when engaging in this sort of gamesmanship, that you make a clear distinction between obviously relevant work-related limitations and incidental quirks or negative attitudes that may be blown out of all proportion in the interviewer's mind, even though they will not prevent you from doing a thoroughly commendable job if you're hired.

Having disposed of the negative side, we now turn to the best way to sell what you do have. While our previous discussion dealt primarily with the techniques of saying something that you would really rather not say at all, the key factor in presenting the positive side of your abilities is knowing precisely what to say. Content is the all-important ingredient to a successful presentation, and technique is secondary.

To see why this is so, recall that we have previously alluded to the undeniable truth that your professional life consists of an enormous number of facts, experiences, and perceptions. No interviewer, no matter how skilled, can possibly get it all. He is, therefore, limited by time constraints to obtaining only a small fraction of the data available from which he will have to make an extremely important decision. Your task, and it is not a small one, is to ensure that every word you say has maximum impact, in terms of convincing the interviewer of your suitability for the position, and maximum relevance to the forthcoming decision.

Keep in mind that your time is precious. Aside from the necessary pleasantries at the beginning of the interview and any peripheral comments the interviewer may make—to which you, in the interest of being personable, should make some reply—you must use this precious time to fill the interviewer's head with facts, experiences, data, perceptions, attitudes, and other things of this nature that will lead him to decide that you are the ideal candidate. Regrettably, many people do not keep the goal in mind when they are seated before the hiring manager. This frequently results in an interview that is more of a visit than a working meeting. Should this occur, the outcome will likely be less information in the hands of the interviewer, and consequently the decision about whether to hire you will be based on a proportionately greater amount of guesswork. If you are matched in the interviewer's mind with an equally credible competitor, the marginal effect of the amount that he or she knows about each of you will be very great.

If you are a person who shops before making a major purchase like a television set, just think over your own experience. Do you not feel much more comfortable purchasing a product about which you know a great deal than investing in one about which you know little? Quite frankly, the magazine *Consumer Reports* is the very embodiment of this preference on the part of almost anyone who is about to spend a lot of money on something hi-tech or otherwise complex and therefore hard to evaluate. Remember this: Without any attempt to be patronizing, whatever you may be otherwise, to the hiring manager you're a product—doubtless one of several— among which he or she will have to choose.

Let us begin with the supposition that the interviewer is quite talented and knows what questions to ask and how to ask them. He or she starts by requesting information about your experiences in high school. The average candidate will respond by thinking back to those years and coming up with one or two general statements from what he can remember. This may be adequate, but it is certainly nothing like intelligent tactics.

On the other hand, the wise candidate will recognize that the interviewer asks these questions in order to find out specific things. Most notably, he will be seeking indicators of (1) stability, (2) industry, (3) creativity, (4) imagination, (5) a desire to participate, (6) preferences as to course material, (7) degree of work orientation, (8) aptitudes, (9) likes and dislikes, and so on. Obviously, it's not likely that he will probe your high school career exhaustively enough to cover all these points. Remember his time constraints. The fact is, he may be going after one or several of these things because that's the way his mind works and he's decided they are important to the final decision. Unfortunately, you don't know what he's really after, because talented interviewers usually phrase their questions so as not to give it away. You can't very well ask what he really wants, because that would be, well, tacky. Your only hope, then, is to produce as much positive information related to these previously outlined points as you can, in the hope that you will hit one or more of his "hot buttons" with your responses. Thus, the question of high school cannot be taken lightly. Your answers must be thoughtful, pointed, comprehensive, and relevant. That's why it's an excellent idea to go over certain features of your background about which you can be virtually certain there will be questions. With such preparation you can produce a quality response without appearing to be hesitant.

Remember, if you have to think too hard in the interviewer's presence to come up with an "on target" answer, you give the game away immediately. He will know that you are tailoring your answer to meet his perceived wishes. The trick is to make your response appear sufficiently spontaneous that the interviewer never really guesses how much thought and calculation went into producing the answer. It cannot be stressed too much. You know ten thousand things about the years you spent in high school. The interviewer will only learn a small fraction of what there is to know. Your task is to insure the sales value, the comprehensiveness, and the relevance of what you actually get to say.

We have picked high school in this instance because it's an experience that everybody shares, although it's unlikely that an interviewer will devote much time to it. Nevertheless, these instructions regarding the quality of your answers apply to every aspect of your experience, particularly that which relates to your career accomplishments.

Résumés, because of their enforced brevity, typically are filled with generalities that sweep over your history with tight little paragraphs designed to arouse interest in the broadest possible audience. This is appropriate for a direct sales piece (which a résumé indeed is), but it is wholly inadequate as an approach for the interview itself. The hiring manager with a clear picture of what he wishes to learn from you will be interested in exactly what you did and precisely how you did it. Those with even greater discernment will be interested in the deeper subject of why you did it that way. Keep in mind, however, that the desire to learn something is not equivalent to the ability to get the information. Many hiring managers with a very clear idea of what they want simply do not have either the experience or the temperament to ask the questions that will get them what they need. As a result, they may ask questions to which the broadest generalities may be applied and still leave the questioner with the feeling that he got a good answer. That sounds wonderful, because you have skipped the hard work of making the scope of your abilities absolutely clear while at the same time pleasing the interviewer.

This is a dangerous deception which does not become evident until you have left the room and are no longer in any position to influence events. At the point when the entire situation goes totally out of your control, the hiring manager will sit back in his chair and begin to reflect on your discussion. As his mind begins to dwell on what he wanted to know and what you actually told him, the awful realization comes that, although he asked a number of questions which he thought would produce decision-making quality answers, the sad fact is that he has generalities which don't give him that peculiar, internally generated confidence necessary to proceed with making a job offer.

If all the candidates he has seen for this position have been equally vague, your own lack of precision will do you little damage, since whatever decision he makes will be largely guesswork. However, should some well-prepared candidate give him the specifics he really wants about job performance, your chances will be harmed to the extent that other things are essentially equal. Remember, these differences in perception occur at the margin, but when you are being compared to similarly bright and experienced people, the marginal things may be the difference between a good offer and a rejection letter in the mail.

The key in these situations is to be very specific. If it's true that a résumé is most effective by being general in nature so as to arouse interest in a broad spectrum of potential employers, it is equally true that the interview is most effective when your experience is described in terms of actual events, activities, projects, and problems. It is easy for a person to say that he or she has extensive experience in property management. The interviewer who does not seek expansion on the statement has nothing but the perceived honesty of the candidate to back it up. On the other hand, if you tell the interviewer, in detail, about the $2 million reroofing contract for which you were completely responsible, he should conclude, after your description of the proposal process, contract awards, work-in-progress reports, personal inspections, engineering meetings, and the like that you know what you're talking about.

As in the case of asking many questions about your prospective job duties, it is virtually impossible to irritate a hiring manager with even a very lengthy description of the tasks you have been assigned and how you handled them, provided that what you say is relevant and informative.

The ultimate challenge, as you may perceive, is to couple the need for this extremely concise and direct information with the scenario in a previous chapter, wherein the interviewer wants the information but has no idea of how to get it. When the "most deadly question" syndrome arises in this context, it will take all your skill to produce a genuinely satisfactory answer to a question that is never even asked. Remember, it is your task to get the information into the interviewer's head, whether he specifically requests it or not. There are no excuses or recriminations against an incompetent interviewer available to you. It's not like a criminal case where, if you have a defense lawyer who doesn't do a good job, you can request a new trial on the grounds that you weren't defended properly. In the hiring game, the bottom line is that you either get the offer or you don't. Once the interview is over, there is precious little you can do to influence the decision.

The ultimate outcome of this discussion is that you really need two written documents related to your career if you wish to seek a professional level job properly. One is your résumé, the direct sales literature which is used exclusively to get you the interview in the first place. The second, however, is sort of a script describing in detail the things about you that must be emphasized to the hiring manager in order to create the most favorable impression. This script should consist primarily of words, phrases, and facts, as opposed to a narrative. After all, you don't intend to read your "lines" as an actor does; rather, you intend to commit the facts to memory in such a way that they can be reeled off in the context of a spontaneous narrative in the interview. If the script contains all the material that you believe is essential for the interviewer to know, and you can, during the course of the interview, mentally check off the items that you have managed to deliver, you will be following a well-organized, extremely effective game plan about which the interviewer knows absolutely nothing but which will immeasurably increase the effectiveness of your presentation.

Some people, with a genuine determination to receive job offers in exchange for their investment of time and effort in the interview process, will prepare a different script for each company they are scheduled to meet, using what they know about the industry, the scope of market, and the business environment they expect to encounter as keys for bringing in additional relevant information about their experiences and abilities.

The ideal arrangement, of course, is a home computer with a good word processing program wherein the script can be modified to suit each new situation with little effort. The printout can then be read, committed to memory, and delivered in a slightly different way for each interview. It is impossible to overestimate the impact that a well-prepared but apparently spontaneous candidate can have on a hiring manager. Remember, the hiring decision is made on the basis of appearances and, to a lesser extent than many people think, some empirical evidence, including reference checks. The more qualified you appear, the greater the likelihood that you will be selected to receive a job offer.

8
Pitfalls for the Unwary

There is one question which reputedly fills most job candidates with dread. It is the legendary "Tell me about yourself." After all, that's not even a question!

You can readily see how a person who is not prepared might freeze when presented with the opportunity to go in any one of a thousand different directions and say anything at all about himself or herself. In the interview, of course, it is too late to begin mapping strategy. For unprepared candidates, this particular suggestion on the part of the employer's representative is a chief cause of sweating palms. You, however, having thoroughly digested the contents of the previous chapter and put on paper a brilliant game plan, will be able to inwardly chuckle at this blessed opportunity to fire your heaviest artillery in the sequence you choose at the most important targets. It is the job interviewing equivalent of a blank check. Nothing will make you look better to a hiring manager than to respond to such an invitation with an apparently spontaneous but clearly well-thought-out narrative of your experience, accomplishments, and career aspirations. To him or her, you will be an impressive candidate, indeed.

Most interviewers, unfortunately, are not quite so accommodating. They proceed with the question-and-answer format and, after years of doing it over and over again, aided by reading some of the numerous books on the subject, they have come up with some interesting gambits in the process. Added to this are the pitfalls which accompany some very obvious and seemingly routine questions that you may be asked. It is to these difficult and dangerous aspects of the encounter that we now turn.

One of the common banalities of the interview is the questioning sequence about your strengths and weaknesses. Everyone naturally rejoices at being asked about their strengths and they will typically reel off a long list of virtues, describing them in loving detail, all the while believing they are making an indelible impression upon the hiring manager. I have found, however, that most hiring managers regard the strength question as relatively unimportant, except that it sets the stage for the question in which they are really interested, "What are your weaknesses?"

Most of them will wearily forbear while the candidate describes his intelligence, her ability to get along with people, his communicative skill, her analytical skill, and so on. They are invariably waiting for this to be over so that they can ask the "flip side" ques-

67

tion without seeming too abrupt. After all, the hiring manager does want to know the candidate's weaknesses. But it would seem somehow socially indelicate to ask only about that. The obvious thing, then, is to create a plus and minus scenario; first the strengths and then the weaknesses.

I say this as preparation for the following advice: Don't give a lot of time to statements about your virtues unless they can be described with specific examples of their application or verified by checking with your superiors at previous places of employment. If you wish to state that you are highly intelligent, you had best bring along some test results to back up the words. If you wish to declare your superior communicative abilities, bring along copies of some of your written memos or reports that were praised by a consensus of managers who will not object to repeating that praise in a reference check. Anything that cannot be backed up in a manner similar to this is called, in the jargon, "blowing smoke." Hiring managers seem to regard the practice with emotions that range from tolerance to, in the case of unrepentant braggarts, intense irritation.

A good idea for making mention of your strengths is to indicate what readily transferable skills you have acquired in recent positions. Some skills, obviously, are relevant only to a particular industry or discipline. Others, however, can be transferred to new applications with relative ease. If your job is, let us say, financial analysis, it may not be clear in the course of describing your duties that you are required to chair a significant number of meetings. This is an excellent thing to bring up at this time because that particular strength is relevant to many different applications of your basic talents, and the ability to run a meeting well is possessed by relatively few people. There are many other examples, but you get the idea.

Now we come to what the hiring manager really wants to know, which is your weaknesses. To this question, it is my experience that the vast majority of otherwise intelligent candidates will respond with such pure nonsense as, "I work too hard" or "I'm too aggressive in pursuit of getting the job done." When the hiring manager hears this, he knows it's time to get out the old hip boots again, and the more apparent sincerity with which it is offered, the more irritated he will get. The fact is that you, just like everybody else, have weaknesses, some of them perhaps rather serious, that impinge upon your effectiveness in the workplace. The hiring manager knows this, and you know it too. In my judgment, you cannot do yourself any good by sheepishly looking at the interviewer and saying in response to this question, "Gee, I can't really think of any, offhand" or some other ridiculous variation of this obvious falsehood. You know as well as he does that if he asked your boss the same question about you in the context of a divine immunity from any consequences to said boss for telling the unvarnished truth, your friendly interviewer would get an earful! Were it not for the growing litigation brought against managers who give truthful but negative references, such checks would be a lot more useful. As it stands today, though, many companies are so afraid of such lawsuits that they won't say anything bad about any former employee, no matter how totally useless a given one might be. This state of affairs works somewhat in your favor, provided you don't allow it to induce you to lie about yourself. My experience is that liars invariably get caught, and when that happens, they get fired.

It is equally foolish to use words that pretend strengths are indeed weaknesses ("I work too hard." Come on!) or to solemnly describe weaknesses that are totally insignificant ("My desk isn't always very neat"). This is an opportunity for you to be much more sincere than other candidates and, at the same time, make points doing it.

Before you ever enter the interview room, you must evaluate yourself and identify two or three genuine weaknesses in your work habits or personal discipline which you can discuss. The thing to keep in mind, however, is that these weaknesses should be real but not sufficiently debilitating to cause the interviewer to doubt your ability to do a good job.

Obviously, a person whose weaknesses include the fact that he is a falling-down drunk will doubtless find that this revelation made to the hiring manager will have some impact on his appraisal. Readers with that particular problem are not encouraged to volunteer such information, although my suggestion truthfully is that they solve their alcoholism before attempting to find a responsible position.

But let us say you are a procrastinator, as most people are. This is a legitimate thing to bring up and, if you word your narrative properly, it can be made to appear both very genuine and, at the same time, not severe enough to materially affect the quality of your on-the-job performance. The same is true for a weakness such as becoming emotionally involved with the personal problems of your staff. Here again, what you say specifically is important because the basic premise can be taken in many different directions. It is one thing to empathize with your subordinates' personal difficulties and thereby perhaps carry more of an emotional burden than a colder manager would. It is quite another to phrase your discussion of this subject so as to suggest that you are the office psychiatrist and rarely get any useful work done. Remember that the words you say will convey a much more powerful impact in the interview than would the same words spoken in another setting. The need to evaluate every possible piece of data before making a crucial hiring decision will cause the interviewer to analyze everything you say. This means *you* had better analyze everything you are *about* to say before you say it. I have known of instances where otherwise capable candidates have literally destroyed themselves with two or three ill-advised sentences in the wrong place. The sad fact is that there is very little room for error in these situations.

To sum up, every job candidate knows intuitively that the revelation of his or her weaknesses will be detrimental to the chances of getting a job offer. Knowing this, most of them respond as I indicated at the outset, either with a description of weaknesses that may be just as easily regarded as strengths or by making the even sillier observation that they have none. The thing which will set you apart positively in the eyes of the hiring manager is that you will be honest, describing genuine weaknesses which will nevertheless not be couched in such terms as to suggest they will seriously hamper your effectiveness, and you will be exhibiting the unusual strength to confront an important but obviously uncomfortable subject head on. If you can turn the discussion of your personal limitations into a selling point in this fashion, you will indeed be ahead of the game.

As you move along, you will doubtless be asked why you either left your most recent position or are considering leaving your present one. This will typically evolve into a discussion of your current or most recent company and the calibre of your superiors. A number of pitfalls lie in this area as well, most notably the tendency to belittle that situation with more vigor than might be prudent.

It does not matter if your superior is a hopeless alcoholic, incapable of writing his own name, much less getting anything useful done, you still cannot badmouth him without encountering possible serious repercussions. If your current company is buying red ink by the barrel and you therefore have a well-founded fear that it may not be around for long, the tendency to go into this in detail with your prospective employer must also be resisted.

To see why this is so, consider that the hiring manager is not only seeking information on sensitive topics here but also trying to discover what kind of person you are when dealing with these subjects. If you are casually negative about your existing superiors, what might you then say about other people in a business setting? If you are indiscreet with sensitive information about your own company, what might you unwisely reveal about this new firm should they hire you in a position where you have access to confidential material?

It is amazing how many otherwise intelligent people will discuss these questions relating to their superiors at their current place of employment with the kind of openness usually reserved for talks between close friends. They somehow have the totally unfounded belief that what they say to this prospective boss is confidential and that it will not be discussed outside the interview room. As a matter of fact, nothing could be further from the truth.

Many prospective employer representatives are even so ignoble as to tell a job candidate that the conversation is confidential as a means of inducing them to talk more freely. These devious people have no intention of honoring their promise of confidentiality and will do whatever is necessary to get the information they want, including giving you a false sense of security about what you're about to say.

The only safe course under these circumstances is to assume that the person you are speaking to has the world's biggest mouth and there exists every likelihood that the things you say about your current employer will somehow get back to him. This is not to say that it will, but you must proceed on the assumption that it might and structure your comments so as not to produce an unpleasant reaction on the part of any third party who hears your characterization of your present employer and superiors. It is far better to err on the side of reticence, so that, even if what you hope never occurs does indeed happen, namely, that your current employer finds out that you are "looking," at least you will not have said anything to enrage him and create a genuine eagerness to give you the boot immediately.

Nevertheless, you must offer a real and compelling motivation to leave your present company if you expect to make a maximum positive impact upon the hiring manager. I am always leery of job candidates who express interest in a position, discuss their background at length with me and my client, but can somehow never come up with a solid reason to leave their current employer. Very frequently it turns out that these estimable folks are seeking, not a new opportunity, but a credible job offer which they can wave in their boss's face and then demand more money or a promotion, secure in the knowledge that if they don't get what they want they can leave with a minimum of fuss. Hiring managers are at least as smart as I am, and many times a good deal smarter; they know these things go on and, again at the margin, they will prefer to make an offer to a candidate who has expressed a well-founded reason to leave her current job than to one who offers vague generalities about advancement and lack of creative opportunities.

In a nutshell, then, your task in this respect is to plant in the interviewer's mind the idea that you really want to leave your current position for good reasons; reasons sufficiently strong to keep you from responding favorably to any counteroffer your existing employer may make once he knows you're about to leave. At the same time, however, you must not couch this narrative in terms that are excessively demeaning to your boss or your company, lest you give the impression that your lips are too loose to be entrusted with sensitive information. Again, the idea of having an outline of what you wish to say committed to memory is recommended when approaching these delicate topics.

Another area of questioning full of dangers for the unwary is the discussion of future goals. The interviewer will typically ask, sweetly, something like, "Where would you like to be five years from now?" or "What do you want out of life?" or "What are your long-range career plans?" There are a lot of reasons for asking questions like this, but one of the most important is that it helps determine a prospective employee's likely longevity with the firm. The wrong answer here can turn a good interview sour in a hurry.

There is no more striking example of what this can do to your chances than an authentic experience I had several years ago with a very fine candidate for a manufacturing firm. He was impressive to all those who spoke to him, he did well on their personality and intelligence tests, and the company seemed ready to make a very attractive offer. But because this was a rather young man with only three or four years of job experience, the question came, "What are your goals in life?"

To this the candidate responded with all candor, "I want to be an air traffic controller."

You can imagine the magnificent effect this had on the interviewer. The company was obviously not offering a job in air traffic control, nor did it ever seem likely that they would be able to fulfill these desires. The upshot was, of course, that he didn't get the job because his goals were inconsistent with what the company could offer.

That hapless candidate indulged himself by responding to a serious question with a blue-sky, "Gee, wouldn't it be nice," "If I really had my 'druthers" approach. In fact, he was a young manufacturing manager who, in all probability, never went to air traffic control school and indeed remained in the field of manufacturing. But because he could not see the purpose behind the question, he fell into the trap of engaging out loud in some wishful thinking and thereby lost an excellent opportunity.

You, on the other hand, must not be so foolish. Never think that any question asked you in a job interview is anything less than goal-directed and relevant to the decision. With the exception of some pleasantries alluded to previously, everything that comes from your mouth should be goal-directed to influencing that decision in your favor. At no place or time in the interview is wishful thinking or speculation appropriate.

You can respond to this type of question both honorably and wisely by simply making a small mental adjustment in the question as it is put to you. If the question is, "Where do you want to be five years from now?" you should mentally rephrase it to say, "Where would I wish to be five years from now if I were employed for a full five years by this company?" If you are seeking a sales management job with an equipment manufacturer, you might express your long-term interest in the equipment manufacturing business and say that you would like to be a vice-president of sales five years hence or a regional director or something, depending upon the size of the company. By silently calculating what two promotions might produce in your status over five years, your answer will then be consistent with what the company can offer and will illustrate to the interviewer your desire to make a long-term contribution. Again, I stress that honesty is important in the makeup of these answers. If you do not wish to be a vice-president in the equipment manufacturing business, you should not say that you do. Then, however, the question becomes why you are wasting everybody's time by taking the interview.

Equally important in the company's perception is the degree to which you seem confident of your goals and determined to achieve them. When the question produces vacillation or hesitancy, the company representative will begin to wonder whether you may not be so uncertain of yourself that in a short time your goals will change altogether and the hiring manager will have to go through the joyous process of replacing you.

High on the list of a hiring manager's dislikes is making a decision, training a new person, and then losing that individual before he or she has been able to accomplish anything significant. Not only is her investment in time and money wasted, but also she must face the prospect of going through the whole thing over again. Any indication from you that this is likely to happen will severely affect your chances of receiving an offer. In general, the hiring manager will prefer a marginally less qualified candidate who she believes will remain with her over a marginally more qualified applicant who she has reason to believe may not be interested in a long-term commitment.

There are variations on this theme of which you should be aware. Influencing factors are age, salary, and industry consistency. A 50-year-old candidate who has spent 20 years in the office supply business and is now making a $60,000 salary must have much stronger internally consistent goals than a 25-year-old seeking her second job after leaving college. The more money you make, the less credible your desire to make a drastic change in either industry or discipline. Likewise, the type of expertise you have will be a factor in that it is generally easier for, say, an accountant to switch industries than a plant manager. After all, financial statements and budgets are remarkably the same in a great many industries, but hi-tech manufacturing is a far cry from putting together wooden chairs.

One final point on this subject is that your goals must be realistic. If you have made an accurate and nonsentimental evaluation of yourself and your talent, certain things will be apparent. A 25-year-old trainee should not try to impress an interviewer by saying that in five years he wants to be president of the company. Neither should a 40-year-old accounting manager who has been in the same position for the last seven years and earns $25,000 a year suggest that *she* expects to be president of the firm in five years either.

Reality must govern here, and you should recognize that, as much as we may regret it, most of us are not superstars. Unless your track record is clearly superior in every way, don't try to pass for one. If you have a very ordinary job history (as most of us do) but think it clever to persuade the interviewer that you are indeed one of "the few," think again. The interviewer will immediately recognize that your assertion is ridiculous, and all the credibility you have built up will go right out the window.

One other thing. It may seem almost too obvious to mention, but I have interviewed a number of people to whom it is not obvious: Never tell a representative of a company thinking about hiring you that your goal in life is to own your own business. Companies, for some reason, have a distinct aversion to hiring and training those who announce in advance that they will one day be their competitors.

A few other topics come to mind for which there are no pat answers, but you should be aware that these things come up regularly in interviews, and you need to have some idea of how to deal with them.

You must be prepared to answer questions dealing with your philosophy of life, of management, of business. They may seek out your attitudes toward delegation of authority, toward having to fire someone, toward capitalism itself. By examining your own mind prior to the encounter and reflecting on these likely questions, your ultimate answer when the question is in fact asked will be much more impressive.

A couple of other areas are also critical and the answers you give will require some thought, preferably before you meet your interrogator.

One particularly strong question is "Why have you been successful?" and you should answer it with something concrete rather than just the standard recitation of your intelligence and communicative ability and the like. This is an opportunity to bring out the strongest feature of you as a professional, and it should not be thrown away. Likewise, a question such as, "What have you learned about business in your career?" can produce a mushy, general answer that will satisfy neither of you, or a clear concise statement of how your wisdom has increased in critical areas. Again, the key to being able to handle these things is knowing yourself beforehand and having some idea of what you will say if the question actually comes your way.

If we seem to have belabored this subject, it is for good reason. Interviewers and hiring managers, particularly at large, well-run companies, are picky. They are fickle, and it does not take much to turn a good interview in the wrong direction. Almost every company representative with whom I have discussed this subject has told me that, in the interview, they are looking for reasons to turn the applicant down, not for reasons why he or she should be hired. They have precious little with which to make a crucial decision except the quality and the responsiveness of the answers they receive in the meeting. To reiterate, it is a tense experience; they are evaluating you every second, and when the interview is over you will be compared to others who have gone through the same process.

Finally, remember this. The decision itself will be made on the basis of everything but the facts. In the immortal words of one hiring manager, "You know, it's just what hits you." You have got to make sure that you are the one that "hits them" just right if you expect to receive an offer.

9
The
Stress Interview

We could have made this volume much more entertaining by dwelling at length on the various kinds of interviewers you are likely to meet. There are so many styles and approaches that another couple of hundred pages could have been included. But the fact is that individual interviewers do not fall into any convenient categories and, even if they did, their personal idiosyncracies would be so numerous that you could not make practical use of the information. Every interview is a unique encounter, and therefore it's impossible to tailor beforehand your tactics by pigeonholing the type of person you are about to meet. The variety is simply too great, and besides, you will have plenty to think about if you have crafted a game plan and committed to memory those aspects of your career experience that seem most likely to be impressive relative to the position for which you are applying.

There are, however, two kinds of interview that are sufficiently different from all the rest that they deserve special mention. The first is called the *stress interview*.

The stress interview is rightly named because, instead of the interviewer and interviewee chatting along in an amiable fashion, the encounter is designed to make the candidate ill at ease from the very start. There is a fair amount of truth in the statement that you don't know a person until you have a problem with him. Believing this, many companies decide that if they cannot know a job applicant in a pleasant meeting, perhaps they can make him or her let something slip in an unpleasant one. Hence, a stress interview.

There are very few people who know how to conduct a stress interview well. This is because it requires either a superb actor who is relatively indifferent to the emotion generated by such an encounter or someone who genuinely likes to make people feel bad. For example, I know one company that has a senior line officer whose very life is made more exciting by the prospect of destroying job candidates that the company deliberately sends into his presence to see whether they can survive his brutal, insulting interrogations. My suspicion is that this firm loses as many qualified people as it gets because his style of interviewing can definitely backfire. A truly impressive person subjected to such treatment may come through with flying colors and then indignantly turn down the job offer based on the unpleasantness of the experience.

I have, however, seen another gentleman who is president of a large investment firm, who personally conducts stress interviews that are emotionally exhausting for the candidate, but then is such a skilled manipulator of people that he can turn around, offer them some appropriately phrased compliments, apologize for his behavior, extend the offer, and receive an acceptance. Clearly, if somebody is that good at stress interviewing, it is a worthwhile tool and should be used.

The danger here is that many companies employ the technique in the belief it will elicit something special from the job applicant but do not have anyone on staff sufficiently skilled to do it in a way that doesn't destroy the applicant's interest in the position once the offer is made. Nevertheless, I suspect stress interviewing is here to stay, and thus you must know how to deal with the situation when it arises.

The first thing to know is that it involves artificial belligerence on the part of the interviewer. This person cannot really dislike you when you are a total stranger and apparently met with some approval in the earlier portions of the evaluating process; therefore, the key word in this context is "artificial," and it is a word you must keep in mind throughout an encounter of this type. In most cases the person assigned to the task will not like it but has to carry out his superior's orders. As I said before, the rare exception is the person of such sour disposition and personal animosity that he or she revels in the opportunity to put down others. May I say that if you sense such to be the case with your stress interviewer, think long and hard before accepting any position with that company, particularly if the person wields any sort of authority. The job may well be open because he's driving everyone else out.

Typically the meeting will not begin on a sour note; there will be the usual smiles and handshakes, invitation to sit down, and some preliminary pleasant questions. Then, however, things will begin to heat up in earnest and you will find yourself in an extremely unpleasant position which you can't get out of without blowing your entire opportunity in the company.

There are a couple of signs regarding this type of encounter that may help put you on your guard. The first is a growing demand on the part of the interviewer that you justify all your actions. When the question "why" starts coming at you with increased frequency and the tone of voice behind it becomes more and more accusatory, you should begin saying to yourself that this may indeed be a stress interview. Obviously, nobody telegraphs the fact that the meeting is going to be a difficult one. The idea of the stress interview is to deceive the candidate into believing that a pleasant meeting is in the offing and to further deceive him into believing that it has somehow gone sour, putting him totally on the defensive. As the questions come faster and the tone more aggressive, the employer will begin to get from the candidate what he doesn't want to give them, namely, answers processed by the emotions and not the brain.

The second reasonably sure sign that a stress interview is in progress is the tendency of the interviewer to cast everything you say in the most negative possible light. You may make an answer regarding your educational status, and the interviewer will come back with a paraphrase of what you just said that is loaded with negative implications. This will immediately call forth in you the need to change his perceptions because he obviously has it all wrong. In fact, if it really is a stress interview, your interrogator does not have it all wrong but rather has sought diligently to make the most damaging statement he can that reflects upon your judgment or perseverance or whatever to elicit from you, not an answer, but a retort. For the stress interview to work to the company's advantage, you must be both on the defensive and a bit hot under the collar, regardless of how well you may try to hide it. One or two accusatory paraphrases may simply be the interviewer's manner, but a steady stream of derogatory reflection based upon your seemingly reasonable answers is a solid sign that you are being manipulated.

The goal of this exercise is essentially to make you stop thinking. Any psychologist will tell you that words spoken in haste are invariably ill-advised, poorly delivered, and most often damaging to your cause. Add to the staccato nature of give and take which often develops in stress interviews your own anger at this insulting person treating you this way, and you may deliver answers that bypass your intellect completely. Emotion-laden answers that come in a heated discussion will have no thought behind them at all, and that is what the company wants.

The stress interviewer is, indeed, seeking to have an argument with you; but a controlled argument such that your anger does not become so great that it turns into a shouting match and the idea of any sort of job offer is lost in the torrent of foolish words from both sides. As I said, stress interviewing is an art, and few people do it well.

When it is done well, however, the company gains valuable

insights that they can get in no other fashion. If your interviewer is a master, he will make you justify actions that otherwise might pass unnoticed. He will make you bare your soul as to the reasons why you've done ordinary things; he will get you to reveal your faults and weaknesses and failures in a way that no normal interview ever could. The companies know that while you are thinking clearly and evaluating your words, you have the upper hand in the interview, because they cannot possibly verify the accuracy of all that you say. As mentioned previously, other companies are reluctant to be highly candid in reference checks, and there is simply no time or money available to conduct the kind of in-depth background investigation normally reserved for presidential appointments but which, if used by private business, would frequently reveal startling evidence of many candidates' feet of clay.

It is the company's awareness of their relative helplessness in separating truth from fiction that gives rise to this interviewing technique in the hope that you will let something slip in an unguarded moment, when you're hot under the collar, facing a person who is not an interviewer but an antagonist.

Once you have identified this situation for what it is, there is precious little you can do but continue through with it. After all, if it were an ordinary argument without being in the context of an objective you wish to reach, you could simply walk out of the room. In this case, there still remains an ostensibly attractive job to be pursued and you may in fact be selected to receive an offer. You don't want one deliberately contrived meeting to put an end to your chances. It therefore becomes essential to perceive what is happening quickly and have in readiness a means to combat this turn of events.

The first thing is to recognize the gambit for what it is. Most seasoned negotiators are well aware that the give and take of a business deal typically involves more than the cold numbers of the transaction. There is a good deal of playacting too, and those who have mastered this aspect of the process are usually a good deal more successful than those who haven't.

One can see this principle carried to extremes by observing the negotiating tactics of certain ethnic groups wherein haggling over the price of merchandise involves shouting, hand-waving, and perhaps even a few insults traded back and forth. Observers unfamiliar with the ritualistic nature of all this might conclude that two persons so engaged would be damaging their relationship beyond hope of agreement, perhaps even beyond repair. This, however, is wrong. The same person would doubtless be astonished to see these two hagglers a half-hour later chatting amiably about the day's news or some other subject as if the "argument" had never taken place. Each knew the other was playacting, each accepted his role in the scenario equally, and presumably some sort of deal was agreed to. Where this sort of negotiation originated I don't know, but these ethnic groups seem to find it satisfactory, and perhaps it meets other emotional needs above and beyond the simple business transaction.

I digress with this as an illustration of the playacting principle. In a stress interview the questioner knows he's playacting; you need to know it, too. This is not easy to keep in mind when the person with whom you are having a pleasant talk suddenly seems, for no apparent reason, to become abrupt and accusatory and all your hopes for an eagerly sought job offer are going down the drain.

Upon recognizing that you are, indeed, participating, however unwillingly, in a stress interview, this one thought must remain uppermost in your mind at all times: This is a game. Only by recognizing this fact will you be able to follow through with the tactics essential to preserving your ego in the interviewing process. Keep saying to yourself, "This is a game. He's playacting. I haven't done anything to bring forth this aggressiveness. Here it comes— this a stress interview." In some stress interviews, conducted by a particularly masterful or malicious interviewer, the only anchor you will have is the repetition to yourself of this singular fact, "This is a game. He's playacting. There is no reason for him to say the things he's saying other than that his role requires it."

Having set your mind appropriately to deal with what may become a steadily more unnerving onslaught, you will be able to operate your game plan. The plan itself is quite simple, but it cannot be put into play without the correct mind set. Remember, the stress interview depends upon your being psychologically off balance. It depends upon your belief that you have somehow upset this person and you must now get back in his good graces. It depends upon your responding too quickly, without thinking, and in a way that leads you deeper into trouble. For if you make one mistake, correct yourself, or add something that might be taken negatively, the genuinely seasoned stress interviewer will then become like the popular conceptions of a defense attorney—he will cross-examine you.

He will go back over that one point time after time, asking why you didn't bring it up before, which version is the correct one, why didn't you say that the first time, and a variety of other approaches. By finding a "chink in your armor" the stress interviewer can get you so completely agitated that you begin shouting at him. I have seen it happen, and it's not a pretty sight. You can avoid falling into this kind of trap by repeating to yourself, "It's only a game. He's deliberately trying to upset me, and I'm not going to fall for it."

Having drilled home this point as thoroughly as I know how, the first step is obviously to remain pleasant and calm, no matter what the interviewer says or what kind of questions come at you. You are to be like the willow, bending in a high wind. The strong and sturdy oak tree will snap its trunk in a strong enough gale; willows never snap, they just bend further over. It is almost impossible for one person to create an argument if the other refuses to respond in kind. By making all your responses evenly, carefully, and pleasantly your stress interviewer will literally have nothing to work with. If anything, your responses should be more careful, studied, and clearly thought out in this situation than in others, because the potential exists for him to nastily exploit any errors of fact or decorum you may make.

The second feature to your response tactic is not to let the incessant demands that you justify your actions or inactions in any phase of your work history lead you to overjustifying. Usually, the demand for information which goes, "Why did you do that?" delivered by an individual who appears to be less than cordial will cause a person to attempt a more thorough selling job than is warranted. If you did not graduate from college because you found college uninteresting and decided to go to work, that is a sufficient answer. The more you try to make it sound like a smart move, the deeper into trouble you will get. Most people who have attained the age of 25 years know there are things they have done that were not particularly bright and, given the opportunity, they would probably have done them differently. You cannot make a dumb move sound smart to a stress interviewer by talking about it at great length. This is exactly what his game calls for, and if you begin to play by those rules, you will most certainly lose.

If the interviewer responds to your statement about going to work instead of finishing school with the acid observation that that wasn't very smart, seeing how important college is these days, you have an alternative. You can spend half an hour justifying your decision, giving him all kinds of added ammunition, or you can simply say, "Yeah, I know that now, but back then it seemed like the best thing to do." Freely admitting a mistake which, when taken in the context of your whole career, is not very significant, cannot be considered a sign of defeat. In a stress interview it may indeed be the wisest course.

Third, you must stick to your game plan as outlined in previous chapters. Your goal of putting certain information into this person's head before the interview is over remains the same. The only difference is that it must be accomplished under more difficult circumstances. When the interviewer uses the negative connotation feedback approach, you must correct his outrageous statements in a cool and pleasant tone and continue making your points. If his rejoinder is one of opinion, it may be best to agree with him. If he deliberately makes an error of fact to throw you off balance, correction is the only appropriate response.

Nobody is psychologically immune to everything. The foregoing represent tips to be followed and unfortunately cannot be considered an impregnable fortress that will leave you invulnerable to the shafts thrown by a very skilled stress interviewer. Nevertheless, if you can at least keep your mind on the key features of what is happening, you will emerge from this experience with as little damage to your chances for an offer (and to your ego) as possible. To reiterate, the thing to remember is that the hostility or aggressiveness shown by the interviewer is deliberately contrived and because of this, if you maintain your composure and doggedly make your points as your plan calls for, the interviewer will have fewer occasions in which to get at you and will concurrently feel less motivated to try. Assuming this individual is nearly as uncomfortable as you are in playing this role, you will receive fewer direct challenges if it soon becomes apparent that they have little effect.

There is one final aspect to this type of interview which must be brought up, distasteful though it is. This has to do with personal questions. It may be that your interviewer will be bound and determined to raise your hackles some way or other and, finding the usual techniques ineffective, will resort to asking questions that have no place in a professionally conducted interview of any kind. Clearly, different people will consider different things out of bounds, but everyone knows that there are some things which strangers simply do not discuss with other strangers. The absolute depth of this sort of thing is usually related to sex.

If you are so unfortunate as to get something like this, you will have the greatest challenge an interviewee can get; namely, having to smile and pleasantly observe that you prefer not to answer that question while inside you are striving mightily to suppress the urge to wring this person's neck. Notwithstanding the crudity of his approach, the latter course is never recommended.

If we assume that your interrogator will not go to such extremes, the more delicate issue is what to do when the questions become personal but not totally beyond the pale. If you refuse to answer, you stand some chance of blowing your investment of time and effort with this particular firm. Companies almost never give reasons for not hiring someone. The actual reason, if the truth be known, may in fact involve illegal discrimination, simple personal dislike, or a host of other things that cannot be set on paper without creating a stir. It does not matter what the real reason for your rejection is; you will not find out unless someone in the firm is very stupid, very indiscreet, or both. The sad fact is that, if you make the stress interviewer unhappy with you, for whatever reason, a negative report can be turned in to the other decision makers and you may be excluded from further consideration without ever knowing why.

On the other hand, if you answer some of these irritating questions in the hope of preserving your chances for an offer, you leave the door open wider and wider without knowing just how personal this imbecile will get or how well you will be able to control yourself as the process deteriorates into muckraking. What to do?

There are two overriding facors that should determine your course of action. The first is how closely you will be working with this person should you accept the job, and the second is whether or not he seems to be enjoying himself in making you squirm. Early on, when you begin to notice that you are indeed being led into a stress interview, you must begin to observe your questioner very carefully, much more so than in the normal interview process, where the emotional tone of things is basically calm. You must look for any sign, any hint, any suggestion that this individual is having fun by making you uncomfortable. There are no hard-and-fast rules to make that determination—a smirk, a lack of emotion on his part, a "going for the kill" kind of attitude—all these are indicators and nothing more. You may be dealing with a superb actor or a genuine sadist.

Once you form some opinion on this, and compare that to his power and influence in the company as well as what your relative positions will be, you can decide how far to go with the personal questions business. You don't want to get into a huff over something innocuous, but you also don't want to leave your dignity on his carpet either.

One final thing and we are through with this unpleasantness. Should you be so unfortunate as to get the worst possible interviewer and the worst possible questions, resist by all means the temptation to simply get up and walk out of the room, perhaps after offering some choice comments in the direction of your tormentor. That very action by itself can lose you a contest which up to that point, you have been clearly winning. If you conduct yourself in a thoroughly professional fashion throughout the process, no matter how brutal, every avenue is open to you. You can write a letter to the company chairman expressing your displeasure with the conduct of Mr. or Ms. so-and-so; you can go back to the person with whom you seemed to have the greatest rapport in the process and ask what in heaven's name that was all about and then describe it, or you can even contact some governmental entity and complain to them. Whatever you do, your position is totally justified. If, however, you gratify yourself with the emotional option, your case is weakened considerably, no matter what action you might wish to take.

Telling someone what you think of his ancestry or giving him some suggestions for an appropriate destination upon demise, while it feels good for the moment, will come back to haunt you. There is simply no room for it, and your professionalism will recieve its greatest test when you act accordingly.

You can sit in the chair opposite this person, look him square in the eye, and say pleasantly, "I prefer not to answer that question" twenty times in a row if necessary, and there is precious little he can do about it. Such a response is the only absolutely secure armor you have from an emotional standpoint and, though you run the risk of irritating the questioner, he has put himself on very shaky ground by daring to ask the questions.

I close this rather grim chapter with what I hope are consoling words, those being that stress interviews are not commonplace in the market, and truly sadistic interviewers are rare indeed. Nevertheless, should you ever encounter one of these situations, you will need all the help you can get. The ideas presented here will at any rate give you a fighting chance.

10
The Personnel Department

U p to now we have concentrated on interviews between you and what we are pleased to call the hiring manager, a man or woman to whom you will report directly if employed or who has a major decision-making role in whether or not you get hired. Usually, however, this is not the first interview. Particularly in large organizations, your initial interview will be with a company recruiter or employment specialist of some kind. This encounter is manifestly different from the other and must be handled in an entirely different way to be successful. The strategy, though quite dissimilar, is nevertheless important, because if you cannot adequately deal with this person you may never see the hiring manager at all.

There is no nice way to say this, so I'll be blunt: The hiring manager is an objective to be taken, the personnel manager is an obstacle to be overcome. Personnel people should not chafe at this, because they know their role is that of screening. An incoming résumé is screened for basic qualifications; a personnel department interview screens to be sure that the qualifications presented on paper actually exist in the person who presents it. The hiring manager may insert another obstacle in the form of his or her assistant, who screens to determine that the applicant has the managerial style and temperament that will mesh well with those of the hiring manager and the existing management team. All these are hurdles which will ultimately be vaulted by only three or four successful candidates whom the hiring manager will actually see and from whom the selection will be made. At the very front end of the process, a third-party recruiter may be involved, in which case we become the first obstacle, although oddly enough our role is rarely perceived that way by the public at large.

Given these facts, your strategy is still to impress the interviewer, but not in quite the same way. Two particularly vivid differences come to mind.

The motivation of the people in personnel is vastly different from that of the hiring manager. While she wants to get the whole thing over with and get back to work, personnel exists for this purpose and wants to impress her with the quality of those presented for final selection. Thus grooming, crispness of presentation, and the like are all still important, but the emphasis will be slightly changed. When it comes to the questions *you* ask, the emphasis will change completely.

While the hiring manager will concentrate on what you know

about your area of presumed expertise, your management style, your approach to solving problems, and so forth, the personnel representative will typically not know enough about the job to discuss this at all. In many large companies, individual employment coordinators may each be given ten or fifteen assignments at once, ranging from an operator in the computer room to a senior marketing executive. They cannot reasonably be expected to understand the details of all the professional jobs the firm tries to fill and are therefore mostly incapable of dealing with in-depth discussion of the actual tasks and responsibilities themselves. They do, however, know a great deal about people and what makes them act the way they do in the job market. Since all human beings like to play to their strengths, it is reasonable to assume that personnel representatives will focus on this area, and invariably they do.

If everything on your résumé is reasonably accurate and can be backed up with appropriate references, your tactics in a personnel interview must be directed to making the interviewer feel at ease with you as a person. It is not the critical element of chemistry which has been discussed before, because you may in fact rarely see this individual except at company picnics if you are indeed hired. But what the personnel interviewer wants to understand, first and foremost, is what motivated you to select certain positions and why you left them. She wants to present the hiring manager with an individual who has good reasons for what she does, a person who knows what she wants, a person who, when faced with an unexpected problem, takes a wise course of action, a person who exhibits a history of selecting a place to work in an intelligent way. If you can show this interviewer that you have made logical moves for legitimate reasons, you will have advanced your cause significantly.

This is by no means to denigrate the role these people play. In small- to medium-size companies your first interview may be an immediate encounter with the personnel director. Some of these people ask extremely detailed, probing, and relentless questions, most of which involve value judgments from you. The most powerful question in their arsenal is *why*—Why did you leave that position? Why did you like that boss? Why did you want a transfer? Why weren't you satisfied with your salary? Why couldn't you get along with that coworker? This is not a stress interview. The personnel director is seeking your real motives, not only for what you did in the past, but as clues to what you are likely to do in the future, particularly if you wind up getting hired by her company. An ability to disarm this kind of person, or at least defuse the questions will be of immeasurable help in moving you quickly over this obstacle and into the presence of the hiring manager, which is where you wanted to be all along. Again, the scripting concept comes into play, only this time dealing with these motivational issues. You need to sit down, examine all your employers, or at least the last 10 or 15 years' worth (if your work history goes back that far) and develop for yourself logical and truthful reasons for making the moves you did. As with the stress interview, in some cases you will have made foolish moves, and there is no clever way to get around this other than to admit that such-and-such decision wasn't very bright, perhaps declaring ruefully that you have at least learned something from the experience. It is a rare job candidate indeed who has not made at least one change involuntarily and, if such is the case with you and you had to take a less-than-ideal job to put food on the table, there is nothing wrong with saying so. Far better that than a long contrived explanation about how brilliant you were to take this clearly inferior position which you are dying to leave, a statement which both of you will disbelieve as soon as the words are out of your mouth.

I know one case involving a very talented man who lost an excellent opportunity because somehow he thought there was wisdom in spending 20 minutes discussing the reason he was looking for work. The president of the firm, although impressed with his abilities, was bored to tears, knew he wasn't getting the truth, and consequently lost interest. Had the candidate simply said that he was fired because the company was seeking ways to save money and the job he was doing could be turned over to a less expensive subordinate, the issue would have been resolved in a matter of seconds. Every intelligent hiring manager knows that these things happen. Talented people get put on the street every day, and a little judicious reference checking would determine soon enough whether this person had been fired for incompetence or had been genuinely victimized by an implacable approach to cost cutting.

We are back again to the matter of the unvarnished truth. If you did something dumb, acknowledge it. If you got fired, say it. If you got fired for cause from your last three jobs, you have a problem which a new job will not cure, and you need to reevaluate a whole lot more than your ability to interview.

In addition to your motives for making certain changes, the

personnel department representative will want to know something about the companies you've worked for. Again, in the absence of detailed knowledge of what you actually do for a living, she will feel on safe ground, and company size, organizational structure, and environment are areas of genuine expertise for these people. Essentially you need to talk their language, telling about the way your current employer has arranged management responsibility, the scope of your markets, the type of products you offer, and things of that nature. The key is to keep your comments sufficiently general that the employment specialist feels at home but sufficiently detailed that, when she is presenting you to the hiring manager, she can offer information of substance—data which shows how hard she has worked and how well she has gotten you to communicate who you are and where you've been all these years. By sticking with such subjects as where you were employed and the reasons why you made changes, you will keep the personnel interviewer comfortable with the meeting and, concurrently, happy to be in your presence. This is no mean accomplishment, as we shall see.

Everybody instinctively knows that you have to have good "chemistry" to get a job offer. But chemistry varies considerably with the level of the position the company is seeking to fill, as well as the personalities of different hiring managers. A board of directors seeking a chief executive may not give a hoot whether someone is prickly or egotistical or acts like a wallflower at parties, provided there's a substantial record of accomplishment and the individual is capable of projecting the kind of image the company wishes to have in the marketplace. A lot of chemistry deals with management style, whether there's consensus as to what constitutes a wise investment, and sometimes simply whether the candidate presents an attitude of confidence and intelligence. If you take the trouble to follow my suggestions, these elements of your persona can be brought forth relatively easily in the normal course of the interview, and you can make whatever points you feel are most necessary, depending upon what kind of person confronts you. In the case of a personnel interviewer, your task is much more challenging.

You have to get this person to like you, to like you well enough to "push" you, to like you well enough to lay aside whatever else may be on her desk, pick up the phone and say, "Vicki, I think we've found someone for that financial analyst position. She's got. . ." and off your interviewer will go extolling your virtues to the one individual you most want to have hear them, namely, the hiring manager. This, by the way, is the common scenario even in large companies when the position is not at officer level. All this happens an hour after you have left the premises, of course, but this kind of interchange typically precedes your being called back for a second meeting. Without it, or some variation thereon, you will not be called back and a very thin envelope will arrive at your home some two weeks later, thanking you for your interest in their company, praising your obvious virtues, and so forth—essentially advising you very sweetly that they're not interested.

The personnel interviewer is thus a "living résumé": She can hurt you but not hire you.

Some people ruefully say that the personnel department is like a little branch of the federal government inside every company. It is a pure bureaucracy which by its very nature neither produces nor sells the product or service the company has to offer. It facilitates good management but itself manages nothing. It wields significant authority, but the extent to which that authority is used wisely or fairly is almost impossible to measure. Whether the original analogy is true or not, the sad fact is that many personnel managers measure their career success on the basis of things that have no relation to the growth and profitability of the company, namely, the size of their departments and the size of their budgets. The federal government comparison is rather hard to shake, isn't it?

Some, though not too many, personnel people are in fact little tin dictators who get job satisfaction from pure ego gratification. They relish the power to help or hurt another person's career chances, and in dealing with such individuals you must be very careful indeed. Hence the following section.

While it's true that you must get this person to like you and want, for whatever reason, to introduce you to her superiors, the corollary is also true—you must avoid saying or doing anything to make her dislike you even slightly. If there is a large number of candidates for any given position, the personnel interviewer has almost total authority over your chances. That individual can either pass you through to the hiring manager or simply forget all about you, and the likelihood that the latter situation will be discovered or conceivably corrected is almost nil. Some very large, highly visible companies that are regular targets for equal employment enforcement agency visits keep scrupulous records on every person who applies for a position. In such a case, that which I have described is less likely to occur. But these large companies are the exception rather than the rule, and the government cannot possibly investigate every firm for routine compliance. Since something like 80 percent of the jobs in American industry are with small companies, you have an excellent chance of running into a personnel situation where no controls exist at all.

The preceding sets the stage for a renewed discussion of what kind of questions you will ask when the opportunity to do so is offered. If we assume for the moment that your personnel interviewer does indeed have absolute authority to put you in the presence of the hiring manager or not, and furthermore is largely ego-satisfaction-motivated, then the issue of not bruising that ego becomes highly important. The worst possible thing you can do is ask the kind of questions emphasized in Chapter 5. This individual in all probability will not have the foggiest idea of the job responsibilities, the problems that are bedeviling the department, or the policies and procedures currently in place. As previously mentioned, there are simply too many departments and too many jobs, even in a medium-sized company, for any personnel interviewer to be totally conversant with them all. If you are speaking with a personnel director who has frequent access to line management, this situation may not be quite as bad, and personnel may indeed have a fairly firm grasp of what the job really calls for. But you cannot assume that, because to do so invites disaster if you're wrong.

Picture yourself in the presence of a proud, ego-driven individual who nevertheless makes no external show of it. You begin to ask detailed, linked, highly relevant questions to which the repeated answer is "I don't know." I suggest that every time you force such an answer from such a person, your chances of being recommended for further interview diminish perceptibly. You have made her uncomfortable, exposed her total ignorance, and made it appear that she is somehow not doing a good job. To my mind this is the kiss of death and, failing some explicit, rigidly enforced procedure for preventing it, your résumé and application will go in the trash the moment the door closes behind you. Do I make myself clear?

Not to despair, however. Your session with the personnel interviewer offers some outstanding opportunites to ask questions, provided they are the right ones. Remembering that you are dealing with someone whose expertise is companies and people, much can be achieved.

When the opportunity comes, your first question should be, offered in a pleasant conversational tone, "How long have you been with the firm, Ms. so-and-so?" That's easy for anyone to answer, and it gives an ego-driven personality the chance to talk about herself. You may, depending upon the individual, get a response that lasts three seconds or three minutes. Anything you can learn will be useful.

Your subsequent line of questioning should be designed for varying degree of penetration, depending on how long the interviewer has been with the firm. Although the cutoff point of one year given in the following discussion is quite arbitrary, it may help you decide how much detail to seek in constructing your own questions about the company and the players involved.

My advice is that if the person has been with the firm less than one year, you should follow up with questions that are very general; the sort of thing one might readily learn in an orientation class: size of the company, number of employees, gross sales, how old the company is, who the founder was, the usual boilerplate. If you are particularly clever, if the company is public, and if you have done your homework by reading their annual reports, you can make points by prefacing your questions with statements that reflect such knowledge about clearly established facts and then follow with something related. Another good tactic is to ask your interviewer what she thinks of the company, what she likes about it, what kind of personalities seem to prevail in the firm; the ambiance, if you will. Obviously you will not ask her to offer anything negative, because that may put her on the spot and you are right back to creating a potentially tense situation, which it has been your purpose all along to avoid.

This is about as far as you can go with a personnel official who's basically just screening. Any attempt to probe deeper and learn some of the things discussed later in this chapter will carry you too far from the company's interests, and you run the risk of irritating the interviewer. Since you definitely want this person on your side, any sign of testiness in answering your questions, no matter how slight, is a strong cue to quit. Regrettably, some interviewers don't show their impatience; they just hold it in and let it work against you after you've left the building, just when you most need them to carry your message forward. All I can do is urge caution; if the answers you get start becoming brief and clipped, cut the questions and move to the closing phase. As a rule, I would keep my question-asking down to not more than five or ten minutes unless you clearly have a talkative interviewer who fairly exudes forthrightness.

Many companies, however, have their recruitment system set up so that personnel will conduct an interview immediately prior to your seeing the hiring manager. If you have an appointment already set up with the hiring manager, it's possible to learn quite a bit more from personnel, since your bona fides have been established sufficiently that you will certainly be put in the presence of one or more decision makers. In such a case, personnel should be more accommodating than if you were just being screened initially. Here is where you can really ask some questions, keeping in mind that you must watch for signs that you are overstaying your welcome in the personnel manager's office.

If your interviewer has been with the firm more than a year, preferably more than two or three years, you can ask about the hiring manager.

Some people are very adept at getting others to talk about themselves, even in situations where it is not normal for them to do so. Thus, a person with natural talent at being interviewed could, in the course of the interview itself, learn about the hiring manager's personality and tenure with the company, and so on. Most people, however, are not very good at it and are less than comfortable intruding on the hiring manager's agenda to get this sort of information for themselves. As we said before, the hiring manager has a specific idea of the data she needs, and anything which distracts her from that goal is likely to be viewed less than charitably. I have found that this sort of information does not come forth readily unless the interviewer is beginning to feel pretty good about a particular candidate and is inclined to move toward building a personal rapport by opening up a bit.

Since it is difficult to get hiring managers to talk about themselves but the information is necessary, the next best thing is to get it from your personnel interviewer if she has been with the firm long enough to know the players to some extent. The surface issues regarding the person you will soon meet can be covered readily: duration of employment, where she worked previously, what kind of person she is, what she typically expects from people, how she comes across to strangers.

If you bring forth your questions in a casual, nonthreatening way, it is almost inconceivable that this approach could hurt you and you may indeed learn something useful. Remember that your personnel interviewer is also a stranger to you, and you have no idea how he or she may react to questions of this type. Certainly she will have no problem in sharing the factual, numeric data and, if she tenses up at the idea of making value judgments on someone else's style and personality, you can always drop it and go on to something else. It may be, however, that this person is a genuine gold mine of information and willing to share it. In this case, you can open up a whole line of questioning that will provide you with insight into the character of the decision-maker you are going to see—insights that can have a powerful bearing upon the way you will handle that meeting.

There is nothing sinister or manipulative in all this; it's not as though you will use this information to somehow gain an advantage over the hiring manager—that is not the point. You are attempting to create a situation where you can be as comfortable as possible in the interview. Since uncertainty breeds fear, the more uncertainty you can eliminate, the less fear you will have. If you know that the person you are about to see is a 43-year-old woman with an MBA from the University of Chicago and a major in finance, who has been with the firm three years and was made a senior vice-president last month, you can form some general impressions about what is beyond that door before you go through it. The bottom line is that anything is preferable to total ignorance. This information does nothing for you other than reduce anxiety. I repeat, you cannot use this information against her, nor should you want to. It is nevertheless useful, and worthy to be obtained prior to the meeting. That's what this whole questioning sequence about the hiring manager is for.

Obviously, if your personnel interviewer is the loquacious sort and she informs you, among other things, that the manger is a graduate of Dartmouth and, lo and behold, you are a graduate of Dartmouth, the value of this information is obvious. If you learn that she happens to be quite interested in theater and you did some serious acting in college, there may be some place in the interview where you can bring it up. In these situations, the advance intelligence you gain from the personnel interviewer can be used for a specific tactical purpose.

Having learned what you can about the hiring manager, without appearing of course to be conducting an interrogation, you should shift to another subject about which the personnel officer should have a reasonable amount of knowledge, that being the organizational structure of the company. There will not be many opportunities for you to ask such questions, so this is a good time to find out several things about how the various levels of authority within the company operate together.

If at all possible, you might perhaps offhandedly ask to see a copy of the organizational chart, showing the president, her subordinates, their subordinates, and so on. A quick glance at this document will give you the best possible idea of the pecking order and, more importantly, will show you the place within it occupied by the hiring manager you expect to see. You can, in the same glance, observe the titles of her peers and get an idea (if the chart is detailed enough) of the organizational structure within which you would work if hired.

Failing an actual glimpse of the chart, you will have to be satisfied with some sort of verbal description offered by your personnel interviewer. Since you are essentially asking questions which don't further company objectives, it's likely the response will depend largely on that individual's personality. Again, a person who loves to talk about the firm may give you an extensive analysis of what's going on organizationally. On the other hand, someone who's offered you the opportunity to ask questions more out of formality than a desire to impart information may be a bit brusque. At the very least, though, you should find out who your hiring manager reports to, who that person reports to, who that person reports to, and on up the line until you reach the president. Any personnel manager who has been with the company more than six months knows this information cold, and there is no reason why she shouldn't be willing to share it.

If you sense openness and a willingness to talk, you might ask how long this particular structure has been in place. You may discover these reporting relationships are only a couple of months old, in which case it might be wise to find out what the situation was prior to the change. A major corporate reorganization that has occurred just prior to the company's seeking new professionals is cause for some concern. In such a situation you are well advised to heed carefully the advice in Chapter 14 about how to decide whether you want the job that's offered.

If you don't actually see an organizational chart, you might ask how formal the structure is. Some companies have an arrangement where everything is just sort of understood; others have chart after chart on the subject but may not wish to show them to an outsider until the process is further along. These are just guidelines; you will have to judge in each situation how far you wish to take any particular line of inquiry.

To round out your sequence of questions for the personnel interviewer, you might ask some questions about the company history, particularly if the firm is very private. Obviously, large, household-name companies have a lot of information available to the public, and if you can get your hands on some of it before the first interview, so much the better. But many very good companies are private, and the founding and early history are not well known. You might discover that the firm was "founded" two years ago, and that in itself is worthwhile information.

To end on a positive note, ask the personnel representative about the company's most significant achievements and accomplishments. Anyone who has any degree of company loyalty will feel good about doing a little bragging, and this puts all concerned in the most positive frame of mind.

If your personnel interview has been scheduled as a prelude to a meeting already arranged with the hiring manager, the next step is formal introduction to that person. If your personnel interviewer has been informative, you will have some idea of the individual you are about to meet, and that should lessen anxiety somewhat. You have left the personnel department with a positive impression, appropriate introductions will be made, and you will be moving into the most significant aspect of your visit to the company.

On the other hand, if your personnel interview is in the nature of a prescreening, and you are not guaranteed a visit with the actual decision maker, you should close by taking up the last phase of the sequence outlined in Chapter 11, "Closing In Hard." Your summing up cannot obviously be in the detail you would use with a true hiring manager, but you should stress your interest in the firm and your belief that your experiences and talent would be useful to them. Once you have said that, you need to make appropriately positive observations about wanting to pursue the opportunity further. After that, all you can do is wait and, perhaps two weeks later, if you have heard nothing, call the personnel department back to see what your status is. They will control your destiny until such time as you actually get to see the decision maker. Once the goal is reached, their function is largely logistical, and you need not be so concerned about the impression you make on them, other than standard courtesy and grooming. The information you have gained, however, will be valuable throughout the remainder of your contact with the firm, and may offer some of the best clues as to whether the job is worth taking if the offer comes your way.

11
Closing in Hard

At some point the employer's representative will indicate that he or she considers the meeting over. It may be as blunt as an outright declaration or something more subtle, such as beginning to shuffle papers or standing up behind the desk. You must at this juncture make a quick evaluation of your situation and take decisive action.

If, during the course of the interview, you have been able to ask a reasonably lengthy series of questions about the job duties as outlined previously, there's not much left to do except go into your closing remarks. If, on the other hand, the discussion has revolved exclusively around you and your qualifications, you must at this point interject a desire to ask some questions.

It is hard to believe this request will be refused, in that it is both eminently reasonable and relevant to the process at hand. Once permission has been given, you must launch into that series of questions which really should have been asked sooner—What is the exact nature of the job? What specific problem is the company trying to solve? What will the hired employee be expected to accomplish and in what time frame? and so on. As I said before, these are designed not only to elicit information but also to illustrate your intelligence, work orientation, and any other positive traits that can be demonstrated by asking good questions. Unless the interviewer has read your mind and, without your having prompted him in the least, delivered a thorough description of exactly what the company wants, it is essesntial that you take the initiative and ask these questions.

You must have the clearest idea possible, not of what the employer is looking for in terms of a person, but of what the new employee is expected to do. These two things are by no means identical, and the assumption that they are has led many job candidates astray.

The process used by companies to determine what they need in a prospective employee is sometimes quite scientific and other times little more than guesswork. Size and supposed sophistication of the firm in question are not, as one might suppose, reliable indicators of how much thought goes into drawing up the specifications, either. Some companies that just plain ought to know better turn in a pretty poor performance when it comes to this aspect of candidate selection.

On those occasions when I have visited some of these places and begun my standard questioning procedure designed to elicit the information needed for a proposal, I am somewhat amused at the amazement with which my thorough and rather relentless approach is greeted. Particularly among senior executives, the process of deciding what is wanted can be extremely informal, and when they have to submit to two hours of interrogation on what exactly is expected, in what time frame, how they will judge performance, and a host of other things, they begin to realize that some of the things they thought were essential are not and others which they completely overlooked are.

I point this out so you can see that, just because a hiring manager believes he needs a certain number of years of experience in a certain industry with a certain educational background, does not necessarily mean that those things are essential to adequate or even superior performance in the task at hand. Here again, you don't know how sophisticated his process for defining these specifications is, and he's not likely to tell you. Thus, your only defense is to know what the job consists of and what the employer expects of anyone who takes it. If you did not learn that earlier on in the meeting, you must learn it now or be at a serious disadvantage in the closing.

Once the interviewer has made signals that it's time to say goodbye, it is far less easy to get into a lengthy discussion of this subject, and you will do yourself no good by pursuing it to the point where you can sense the interviewer's brewing impatience. That technique is appropriate only in the circumstance where the interviewer still wants to learn things from you and is essentially cooperating with your questions out of a desire to move the process forward. As mentioned before, if you can get him focused on the problems confronting his area of responsibility and come over to his side of the desk, as it were, to do so mutually, you will have scored some of the highest points possible.

When your questions come before the end of the interview, even if you do prolong your probing, any residual irritation caused by it will be forgotten (provided you didn't push too far!), and the feeling that remains will be an impression of thoroughness and commitment to knowing the job.

This will not work once the interviewer has decided in his own mind that the meeting is over and has begun mentally to move to the next item on his agenda. If you catch him with your questions at this point, he will simply want to get it over with. If you attempt to drag out the questions anyway, with the interviewer in that frame of mind, the most likely residual effect will be aggravation that you are taking up too much time. Your case will hardly be helped and may be seriously hurt if that is the last impression this decision maker has of you.

Thus, if things have been allowed to go this long, you must ask some brisk, highly relevant questions that can be answered quickly. Perhaps the best approach is to take whatever information you have and construct a likely scenario and offer it to the interviewer for his agreement or modification. Whatever happens, you cannot let this process last longer than a few minutes if it comes at the end of the interview.

Once you have, either in the middle of the interview or at the close, developed all the information you can get about the tasks, responsibilities, and expectations involved in the job itself, you are ready to perform the closest thing to a standard salesman's close that the meeting will offer. There are some very specific guidelines on how to handle the last two minutes of this encounter, and proper conduct here will pay rich dividends.

The first thing, and remarkably few candidates remember to do it, is to thank the interviewer for his time. This is a nice gesture that takes just a few seconds and, at the very least, it shows good breeding if nothing else.

After this, a brief recapitulation is in order. The interviewer has asked many questions over the course of the last 45 to 90 minutes, and you have asked a few yourself. The discussion has presumably been far-ranging, and a lot of words have passed back and forth. The interviewer is not about to clarify his evaluation of you in your presence, but it is certainly appropriate for you to make clear your own understanding of the interview in his presence. It is another little-used sales tool that indicates your ability to marshall your thoughts, deliver an impromptu report, and distill a lot of information into its essentials.

If you are a skilled speaker and do this sort of thing with great brilliance, here is the place to show off. The recap must be short but highly concise and with a genuine impact upon the interviewer, illustrating your full grasp of all that has occurred during the meeting. If, on the other hand, your talents do not run to extemporaneous speaking or immediate distillation of essentials from much data, you cannot just skip this step as not applicable to you. You must still make the attempt to sum up the meeting, although perhaps with greater brevity and consequently less detail. Few things infuriate an executive who wants to do something else more than listening to a lot of words that don't say anything. Stay on firm ground, repeating back to him only those things you know are major aspects of the job, leaving the fancy footwork for those with a flair for it. I repeat, you cannot forget the recap—it is essential to your overall strategy, as we shall see.

The first element of this recapitulation is to show that you understand the job. If you have asked the right kind of questions and have received good narrative answers, you should be able, in five or ten well-chosen sentences, to describe the responsibilities involved and what the employer's real need is.

Following this should come a brief statement outlining your most significant strengths and how they relate to what you have just said. At this point you may be able to hammer home the message that, although your qualifications do not meet the exact outline the interviewer has in mind, you are nevertheless eminently qualified to get the job done. Depending upon the political realities inside the company and/or the extent to which drawing up those specifications was a sophisticated process that cannot be easily overturned, the interviewer may begin to realize that you do in fact have what he needs, even though you may lack some of the "bells and whistles" that he was originally seeking. Remember, you have no idea how he arrived at the items on his checklist of desirable features in a candicate. Some very large companies do this with two or three executives sitting around a table tossing ideas back and forth. Some of them are hopelessly unrealistic; some of the things deemed necessary are irrelevant; and sometimes they will find themselves facing the prospect of paying dearly for them when an equally qualified but much less expensive candidate may perform superbly.

If a personnel department is helping develop specifications, the process may become more systematized, but again this depends upon the quality of the department. If a third-party recruiter is involved, the process may become even more refined, although once more it depends upon how well the recruiter knows his business.

While you are thinking of all this, keep in mind that you know nothing of what the company has done to arrive at the candidate specifications. By knowing the job, however, and selling your strongest points to line up with the features of that job, you are doing some of the interviewer's evaluation work for him. This, as most professional sales people will tell you, is the essence of selling. It is not a question of exaggerated claims or high pressure, but rather a simple and clear presentation of facts delivered in such a way as to motivate the buyer to act positively. This second portion of the recap is the most significant selling you will do throughout the meeting. You must clearly outline your strengths and how they relate to the position for which you are applying.

Where the interviewer has, for some reason, indicated the exact nature of the specifications before him, you can easily stress those points where your experience or ability are directly in line with them. If you can get close, present those aspects of your background.

But if you have no idea of the characteristics he's looking for, your only course of action is to use what you know about the tasks that must be performed as a guide for presenting one last time those strengths that appear most relevant to the job at hand. You may not be able to get the interviewer to tell you what he wants in a person, but you can surely get a description of the job and the problems that need to be solved. If you cannot get this in the first meeting, the company is either seriously in turmoil about what is needed, or your rapport with the interviewer is virtually nonexistent. Based on my years of experience, I would say that in such a case very few invitations for a second go-round are extended, to say nothing of offers. If you should get an offer, be wary. Companies that don't have a clear idea of why they are hiring someone may discover in a few months that they don't need him. This unfortunately happens more than one might think; candidates who don't look before they leap can find themselves in a very awkward position. More on this in Chapter 14.

The final rule on stressing your long suit in the manner described is "You may as well be shot for a sheep as a lamb." If the recap is brief and factual, it can hardly do you any harm. It may well stress some point that the interviewer has overlooked or failed to make note of. At best, it may change his mind about what is really needed and put you in the forefront of the contenders for the position.

The third point of the recap is the equivalent of asking for the order. You must be careful here, because you don't wish to seem too eager. At the same time, generating an impression of aloofness will not help your case.

In the heat of battle, many candidates fail to remember that interviewers, employers, hiring managers, even senior executives are people too. Nobody likes to be rejected, and most human beings avoid situations where rejection will occur if they can. The reason the selling profession pays so well, according to some, is that the emotional stress of bearing up under significant daily rejection must be highly compensated or nobody would do that kind of work. If a person could only make as much money selling life insurance as he could being a bookkeeper, I suspect very few people would sell life insurance. As it is, successful insurance sales representatives who can endure the continuous rejection that is part of the business are rewarded with extremely handsome compensation, normally out of all proportion to their level of education or even some theoretically derived determination of the value to society of such employment. The same is largely true for stockbrokers, real estate salespeople, door-to-door sellers of magazines and, yes, even executive recruiters.

Since nobody likes to be rejected, one of your tasks before the door closes behind you is to create in the mind of the interviewer the idea that, if you are invited back, you will not reject the invitation. At the margin, with two candidates priced about the same and having equal talent, the interviewer will invariably arrange another visit or actually extend an offer to the person believed most likely to be appreciative and accept. As the third part of your recapitulation, you must leave the interviewer with the strongest possible impression of your likely acceptance without saying or doing anything to indicate total acceptance.

The reason for this is clear. You want your turn to serve. Once the company has decided that you are indeed the answer to their prayers, the employee of their dreams, they will extend an offer. At that point you will not want to have created in their minds the idea that any reticence on your part constitutes betrayal.

There are not many instances where a stock answer is called for in the interview process. This, however, is one of the few times when such a tactic is effective. There is a phrase which I encourage candidates to use that has just the right mixture of enthusiasm and reticence to make the hiring manager feel confident that his overture of a second meeting or even a job offer will be warmly received but not cause him to presuppose that you will fall into his arms. It goes something like this: "Well, Mr. or Ms. so-and-so, I certainly appreciate the time you have spent with me in discussing this position. It seems like an exciting opportunity and I would like to pursue it further. Can you tell me what the next step would be and approximately when we could move forward?"

With this approach, you offer everything and give away nothing. By expressing your interest in some positive terms such as "exciting", "challenging", "unusual opportunity," you set the interviewer's mind at rest about your potential interest and thereby generate goodwill. By asking to take the next step, you make it clear that you will respond affirmatively to another invitation, and by asking about time frames you suggest ever so slightly that you have your own schedule and that you are not necessarily going to be waiting around forever to hear from them.

While we are on the subject of proper attitude, it should be noted that this will not work very well if, during the course of the meeting, you have had an insouciant manner about you or even used body language to suggest that there is something about this whole thing that is sort of a yawn. As I said previously, hiring managers evaluate everything in these encounters, because they are painfully aware of how little information they will have upon which to make a critical decision. Slouching in the chair, any expression of excessive casualness, the impression that you expect the company to come to you—all will be duly noted, and not in your favor. Your attitude throughout the interview must be one of professionalism coupled with a restrained eagerness that, by design, shows through once in a while to give the interviewer emotional support for a decision to call you back or actually extend an offer.

To sum up, the perfect close from your viewpoint is one in which you can succinctly and accurately declare your understanding of what is needed to fill the position, your expression of confidence that certain specific aspects of your character and background are highly relevant, and an expression of interest in pursuing the matter further without losing your opportunity to legitimately ask some tough questions should the offer be extended. If the hiring manager's final impression of you is largely formed around such a summation, you will have accomplished all that can be expected in a meeting of this kind.

This is not the end, however. It is quite likely that you will be only one of several individuals that this person interviews and, unless you are an extraordinarily well-qualified candidate, the hiring manager will not spend the next several days thinking about you to the exclusion of all else. A little subtle marketing, at this point, will do you no harm.

Approximately one to two days after the interview has taken place, you should craft a brief but thoughtful letter of appreciation to the hiring manager, thanking him for his time, bringing up one or two other points of information which may be particularly useful in your behalf and again expressing the desire to continue the process. There is really no reason for such a letter other than to do a few basic things, the most important of which is to put your name in front of his face one more time.

Hiring managers are busy people and bringing someone new aboard may be important, but it's not the only thing they think about. The hiring process, particularly for positions in senior management, regularly takes from two to three months, and obviously during that time the hiring manager is not sitting around thinking about candidates.

If, however, a crisp, perfectly typed, carefully worded letter arrives with your name on it and conveys some useful bit of additional information, no matter how slight, it will be obvious that you have learned your corporate manners well, that you understand how the interview game is played, and, not insignificant these days, that you know how to produce a quality piece of correspondence. While it is true that your letter may receive only a cursory glance before being stapled to the rest of your file and put away, it is also possible that seeing your name once more may generate warm feelings in the hiring manager and motivate him to set aside some other pressing business and reflect upon you and what a benefit to the company your presence would be. If your letter is that good, it will be well worth the time and postage expended in sending it.

Don't forget that if your visit to the company has involved more than one interview, a letter should be sent to each person with whom you had a meeting. There is nothing to suggest that the one letter you send will be passed around among the decision makers, so several letters emphasizing some significant aspect of your encounter with each person will just put your name in front of the company at large that many more times. In these group decision-making situations, you never know who is going to be your "booster," the person who wants you on the team badly enough to sell you to the others. Likewise, you never know which letter will hit a particular group member just right and create a booster for you. I suppose this is the closest thing to advertising any job candidate does: Getting the name out with a quick positive message designed to induce action.

At this point there is little more than you can do. Once the follow-up letters are sent, the decision rests with the company and those charged with making the hiring selection. In rare cases, if you have learned that a connection exists between one of these decision makers and someone you know well enough to ask a favor, it is possible to request that your friend or colleague contact the one they know inside the company and put in a good word for you. If it is done with subtlety and good taste, this tactic cannot hurt your chances and may indeed be a great help. Aside from this relatively rare opportunity to further your cause, you simply wait.

If you hear nothing in two weeks, you may telelphone the company and ask to speak with the hiring manager who talked to you. If that person is not available, it may be possible to gain some useful information from the department secretary. The greatest likelihood, however, is that you will be told nothing significant; the usual boilerplate offered by secretaries and hiring managers alike is that they are still working on it, or you are still under consideration, or the matter is under review. So you wait some more.

With lower-level positions, it has been my experience that companies wanting to hire move fast. Good candidates are never numerous, and the right combination of talent, experience, and chemistry which occurs between hiring manager and job applicant is not easy to duplicate with another person. There are no hard and fast rules in this regard, but I venture to say that if you are seeking a position that involves relatively limited authority within the company and you have heard nothing in two weeks, the probability is that you are no longer under consideration.

In larger companies, or well-managed medium-sized ones, the decision that you are not appropriate for the opening in question is usually accompanied by the swift dispatch of a brief but pleasant letter telling you so. In small companies, you may simply hear nothing, because there is nobody asigned to write or mail such letters and everyone is so busy just trying to keep the place afloat that it is simply not a priority. Letters of this kind are invariably devoid of any information as to why you weren't chosen; they merely state the fact as diplomatically as possible.

If the position in question involves greater authority or

requires a significant professional skill level, the time frame for a decision is usually much longer. The company, rather than taking the first available candidate who meets their requirements, will select from several, all of whom have been prescreened and interviewed by the hiring manager at least once, perhaps twice. In these instances all the candidates do not necessarily come to the firm's attention at the same time, and therefore the time lag can be considerable. If you are attractive candidate No. 1 and attractive candidate No. 2 does not appear on the scene for six weeks, there is no deception at all in the company's saying that you are actively under consideration, but they have not gotten around to moving further with you even though a month has passed. A good rule of thumb in these cases is to recontact the hiring manager by telephone about every two weeks, seeking to determine whether any progress has been made. If there is any honesty in them at all, at some point you will hear that another individual has been selected or that the firm has "decided to do something else" (if the person you're talking to can't bring himself to say the company has rejected you). Either way, you have the information that you need, and you can move on to more promising things.

Once all the quality candidates have been interviewed, companies will take a long time to arrive at a hiring decision for essentially only three reasons. The first is that some are bureaucratic behemoths where nothing can be done in less than three months, not even requisitioning a box of paper clips. There are many companies like this, and some of them, oddly enough, turn out to be excellent places to work if you can stand the waiting while they process your paperwork through an interminable number of departments, executives, and forms in triplicate. Even so, no reasonable person should begrudge an eager candidate in whom they have a legitimate interest a request every other week or so to see how things are going.

The second reason is that the company genuinely cannot achieve consensus among the decision makers. These situations frequently have less to do with the quality of the candidates than with the political realities inside the firm, a topic about which another whole book could be written. Ordinarily one candidate is a clear standout, but because of power plays the individual cannot be aggressively sought the way the hiring manager would probably like to do if the decision were entirely up to him. You have no control over these situations; this is just to show you what can happen to drag things out.

The third reason that you don't hear anything is that the company really has decided to do something else. Many times requisitions are withdrawn, the company has a bad quarter, the budget will not support the requisition under hastily imposed austerity, and it is simply dropped. Other times, new top management may arrive with different priorities which don't include the new position and again the selection process stops. I have never seen a company send a rejection letter which said, in effect, "We really were going to hire somebody but we decided against it." This is just too honest, and most companies will revert to the standard verbiage about how impressive you are and how they will keep your résumé on file and how there is no further interest at this time. Everybody who seeks a significant job collects a certain number of these throughout his or her career, and they are just part of the game.

In closing this chapter, let us assume that you have fired your heaviest artillery at the most likely targets and, from all appearances, have been well received. You have written your letter of thanks to the hiring manager and must now wait. The question is, what's going on inside the decision maker's head? Let's see if we can find out.

12

The Warm Fuzzy Orange Ball

As we have said, the hiring decision is the ultimate intangible. The buyer is getting a product so complex that he or she cannot possibly evaluate it with any degree of precision. There is so much information available upon which to base a decision that no interviewer can get it all, and there is a high probability that much relevant material will be totally left out. The decision maker can check references, but there is no assurance that the statements made by those people are accurate or even honest, because the question of their motives is another intangible about which there is even less information. It is almost impossible to determine whether a former employer is in fact a close friend who will say anything at all to help the candidate or, on the other hand, someone who knows deperately negative things about the candidate but will not reveal them out of fear of a lawsuit should it be discovered he did so. In such an environment of unknown unknowns and undefinable objectives, the hiring manager must decide.

A candidate with the right kind of schooling and the right industry orientation, who has worked in the appropriate departments and developed skills that should be useful, may or may not convey all these things adequately in the interview. It is entirely a matter of technique, a matter of presence of mind, a matter of strategy, and employing the tactics necessary to carry it out. But those surface qualifications, even if they exist, are not the deciding factors. Everybody who is seriously considered will have survived some sort of screening and will present the same general collection of experiences and talent. That is only the tip of the iceberg.

The hiring manager will make the decision on the basis of what can only be called intuition. In previous chapters I have used some of the phrases I have actually heard employers use to describe why they liked a certain person. In the screening stage, they are objective evaluators of experience, duration of employment, and other factors because they are only screening. But when the time comes for ultimate selection, there are no objective criteria any more; chemistry, appearance, articulation, a winning smile, a firm handshake, good manners, and knowledge of current events begin to take over. The employer is no longer relying upon objective criteria—he is now almost in the realm of the metaphysical.

There is an experience which most people have on rare occasions that approximates what I personally have felt and what I suspect most hiring managers feel when making a final selection of an important employee. Everyone naturally experiences this a bit differently, but I am convinced something similar happens within everybody when the physical and emotional phenomenon that I am about to describe actually takes place. It is the ultimate intangible and will not be easy to convey objectively, but I'll try.

You have to sort of identify with this whole thing for it to do you any good, to see yourself in the following situation, having the experience I hope to illustrate so that you are able to put yourself in the hiring manager's place this one last time.

It happens when things go right—not just a little bit right, but super right. It may be a particularly gratifying telephone call, either because the conversation was pleasant or the news you heard was positive and exciting. It may be that you're finishing up a long and difficult project, but you know you've done your best, and it really is coming together quite well. It may be that you are simply reflecting on a precious moment with another person, or upon your wife or children. It may be that you have just talked to someone who is extremely well qualified and well suited for a position you want to fill.

Then it comes: Maybe it starts in the pit of your stomach or spreads across your shoulders or emerges from inside almost all at once everywhere. It is a physical and emotional sensation at one and the same time. You cannot summon it, but likewise it is almost impossible to stop it. Perhaps people who have dabbled in the drug culture might relate it to the "rush" that comes when taking certain substances into their bodies. But it happens, and it happens in response to a stimulus that is internally generated by an enormous feeling of goodwill, optimism, love, or high expectation. It's what I call the warm fuzzy orange ball.

Now, as bizarre as this may sound, it is actually quite real, and you have to be aware of it because, easily done or not, creating this feeling in the hiring manager is the true ultimate goal for which you are striving. As I've tried to make clear, the hiring decision is an emotional one, backed up by precious few facts and formed almost exclusively through impressions. It is only reasonable, therefore, to suppose that an emotional decision would be most strongly verified by an emotional experience associated with it. I have observed this phenomenon in myself on numerous occasions and, when I've asked executives whom I know well enough to address the subject, their response is invariably affirmation of the reality of the experience in their own lives as well. Not everybody gets this reaction in the same way, of course, and not everybody gets it every time he or she makes a hiring decision. But when they make an unusually good one, my very unscientific surveys suggest that the decision was accompanied by this kind of feeling.

There are no pat answers as to how to make this happen in the person you're talking to. The whole thing is too complex for that. It is likewise hard to sense whether the warm fuzzy orange ball is forming or not, because typically this happens totally on the inside and there are no outward manifestations of it. Nevertheless, elusive though it may be, this is your ultimate target, and you may as well know what you're shooting at. If you can generate this kind of feeling in the hiring manager every time she thinks about you, my conclusion is that you are 99 percent hired if the decision is entirely hers.

One other point is that the ball forms slowly inside a person; it doesn't automatically appear as if by magic. It is not a situation where the feeling is totally absent one moment and appears in full bloom the next. It is rather a formative process and seems to build inside until the individual is actually aware of what is going on within. Particularly in an interview, there will be a series of unusually rewarding sequences where it becomes more and more obvious that the person to be hired is meeting every desirability factor. This growing awareness causes the "ball" to form until it grows intense enough for the person to recognize it. As a summary of what has gone before, we should go over the several points that make for a totally satisfactory interview from the hiring manager's perspective and which might reasonably lead to the experience I've described actually taking place.

The interview must be easy, which means you have to pace it properly, neither making your questioner work too hard or forcing her to sit through long explanations of things in which she has no interest. If she gets all the information she wants and only the information she wants with the least effort, you have fulfilled this aspect of forming the fuzzy ball.

You have to hit the right buttons, meaning that you must address all those things which, declared or undeclared, are important to the hiring manager, and you must do so in a manner that satisfies her as to your suitability for the position in each respect. For a professional position there may be several job descriptions. First there's the long detailed one drawn up by the personnel department, then the one that has resulted from the managers in the department sitting around talking about it after work, and finally the one that usually resides only in the decision maker's head—clearly the most important. In many cases, a well-qualified person may present an aspect of his or her background or ability that causes a sudden sea change in what the manager perceives to be required—the job begins to develop around the candidate's talents, as it were. Hitting all the buttons is not easy, because they are not all exposed and you never know from situation to situation what the percentage is. Some hiring managers have their whole agenda in their heads; others will follow the written outline to the letter, and of course there are hundreds of variations in the middle. You cannot know in advance; the best you can do is learn something about the manager before the visit and attempt to glean a bit from that.

Thirdly, you have to act right. This is a combination of courtesy, appearance, mannerisms, articulateness, confidence, and your overall personality. Obviously you cannot be anything but yourself, and attempts at affectation invariably backfire. Nevertheless, if you behave as if you were in the presence of the President of the United States, you are likely to do a whole lot better than if you behave as though you were at a football game. Remembering your complexity as an individual and that you can present yourself quite differently in different circumstances, you have to adjust your personality and demeanor to suit the situation as best you can. Other than this, you and the manager will either get along or not. Since you don't want to work for someone you dislike, the lack of a job offer in that situation should cause little grief.

Finally, to form the warm fuzzy orange ball, you must present personal career goals with which the hiring manager is comfortable. She must feel that those goals are within the context of long-term employment with her company. She must feel they are realistic for your intelligence level and abilities and those goals must be couched in such terms that, if you are hired, she will be bringing in a new member of the "family." If you're an unusually impressive candidate and she gets the idea that you will be around for awhile, the thought running through her mind will be that every time you do something new that's brilliant, it will reflect well upon her own reputation within the firm. Obviously people are motivated by what will do them good personally, and thus she should receive all sorts of warm feelings at such a prospect.

If your appearance, personality, demeanor, substantive answers, and goals are all consistent with the need that actually exists in a particular situation, you are hired as far as the company is concerned. Whether or not you want the job is something we shall discuss in Chapter 14.

There is another side to this, of course, and that is that just as the warm fuzzy ball can be formed, it can also be blown apart while in the forming stages. Some of these destructive forces you can control; others you cannot. It's worth taking a look at all of them to give you further understanding.

One of the surest ways to disintegrate your little forming ball is to belabor an irrelevant subject. I have seen this happen countless times; a talented person is moving forward successfully in the interview, the hiring manager is responding nicely, the ball seems to be forming as they interact with each other, and then, for some reason or other, the candidate decides to take ten minutes to discuss something which he just feels he must talk about but about which the hiring manager could care less. As the minutes drag on, the ball disintegrates; the candidate has no idea what he's doing to himself, and later it's up to me to inform the person that the company has no further interest.

You may think something like a brief interlude of irrelevancy would not be enough to destroy a candidate's chances. It *is* enough; it has happened time and time again and will continue to happen. Anything which interrupts the emotionally satisfying nature of the interview can be devastating. If you want to squash your little orange fuzzy ball flat, that's the perfect way to do it.

It is not only irrelevancies that can produce this result. There may be a very legitimate aspect of your experience or talent that you wish to stress that can lead to the same negative reaction. Remember that what is important to you doesn't count it it's not important to the hiring manager. For this reason I again urge answers that are relatively brief, creating a menu from which your interviewer can choose a direction. Only when you're confident that you have her genuine attention should you go into great detail. The process of feeding the right information at the right time is a critical aspect of these encounters, and inability to gauge your moves can destroy the feeling of progress which has been developing.

In contrast to what we said earlier, your warm fuzzy ball can begin to disintegrate if your motives and objectives are poorly focused and you leave the hiring manager with the feeling that you don't know what you want. Nothing so infuriates these people as to spend a lot of time and effort selecting and landing a good candidate and then having to repeat the process six or nine months down the road. It's particularly galling when the new employee leaves of his or her own volition. This too can have a negative impact upon the manager's own perceived competence within the company, and therefore a candidate who lacks goals consistent with a long-term contribution to the company may give the hiring manager a considerable feeling of uneasiness. It should be obvious that uneasiness and the warm glow that you are trying to achieve are mutually exclusive; if you have one, you don't have the other.

These features of the interview are more or less within your control; that is, if you do everything just right and avoid doing things wrong, you should get the desired result. There are two other areas which often impact your reception at the hands of a company, and they are, for all intents and purposes, totally outside your sphere of influence. Since we're attempting to discuss the whole system, you may as well know about these, although there's not much you can do about them.

If the hiring manager is having a hard day at the office, she will simply be more difficult to reach than at other times. Most people who do this kind of decision making are not accustomed to adjusting their personalities to situations unless it is clearly to their advantage to do so. Thus, a hiring manager who is tired or not feeling chipper may come on brusque or disinterested and leave you totally flustered, wondering what you've done wrong and why this individual doesn't like you. If she were attempting to sell *you* something, she'd put her emotions behind her, wear a brave smile, and go into her act. But as the hiring manager she doesn't have to do that, and therefore, in many cases, the attitude displayed is simply, "This is how I am today and if you don't like it, so what?" If you run into this, there is no likelihood of forming a warm fuzzy ball that day, and your best bet is, if at all possible, to make the meeting brief and ask for another opportunity to chat in more detail. The manager may be glad to escape or conversely, she may resent your taking charge to that extent. In that event, I suggest it is better to be shot for a sheep than a lamb and if you go through a lengthy interview under those circumstances, not much will be accomplished no matter what you do.

Again, I speak from experience and not research or theory. I know one executive vice-president of a large financial services company who is normally the most affable gentleman imaginable. If, however, business is going poorly on the day an interview is scheduled, he won't cancel it but just go ahead with a very obvious sour disposition. Candidates who are not prepared for this feature of his personality are thrown totally off guard; their game plan goes out the window in a vain attempt to establish rapport, and the whole event becomes a miserable failure. In the past, I have even resorted to finding out how his day is going prior to an important interview and, if things are looking bleak, arranging a cancellation by the candidate and rescheduling so that he will not be at a disadvantage from which it is impossible to recover.

The final "fuzzy ball killer" is similar in that it involves negative distractions during the meeting. Some managers will take telephone calls while an interview is in process. You cannot very well order them not to, and if something happens during one of those calls that is grim or unpleasant, I'm sad to say your warm fuzzy ball will be blown sky high and you will never know it. The reason is that most people, business executives included, are very bad at compartmentalizing their emotions. They either feel good or bad, and very few bother to analyze what is causing the overall feeling. An enormous feeling of goodwill and gladness generated by your extremely positive performance in an interview, can, unfortunately, be blasted to smithereens by a telephone call in which the executive learns that her company's request for a $10 million line of credit has just been turned down. This negative news so seriously outweighs her previous feeling of gladness that the overall effect is that after the call she no longer feels good but terrible. The other sad thing is that, when she recalls your meeting, she may imprint on it the negative emotions generated by the phone call rather than those which would be attributed to your performance. This isn't intelligent, nor logical, nor does it do either of you any good, but it happens. I'm afraid there's no defense for this; I just wanted to warn you that this is one of the problems that you may some day face and it's better to know than to be ignorant.

Keep in mind that this whole discussion represents the ideal. Not every hiring decision is accompanied by such a feeling inside the one making it. It may be fair to say that most such decisions come without the appearance of this unusual emotional verification to make the hiring manager feel certain that this decision is a good one. Nevertheless, those who have had it will tell you that when the warm fuzzy orange ball is in full bloom, there's no mistaking it. The crescendo of the formation process is almost a physical experience and, at least in my case, is remembered long after it occurs the first time. There are even cases where it will recur every time I think of the person or situation that produced it initially, and I guarantee you that if your appearance before a hiring manager produces that kind of reaction every time your name comes up over the ensuing two weeks, the likelihood that you will receive an excellent offer is extremely high.

As a final comment, may I say that this is something you shoot for almost subconsciously. Don't change your approach or your style in an effort to "make it happen" by gauging your interviewer's reactions to each different change in the hope that you will finally hit upon the right one. If you follow the strategies and techniques outlined in this book in a faithful and consistent manner, nothing in the way of extraordinary effort will be needed. It's a bit like baseball; don't try to hit a home run every time. If you keep your eye on the ball, swing properly, and follow through, you should get a fair percentage of hits. The home runs will come by themselves when everything lines up just right.

So it is with interviewing, my friend. If you have the basic qualifications and follow the ideas outlined here, you will get a good number of offers. When everything is just right, you will hand your hiring manager a warm fuzzy orange ball the size of a house, and you will have hit a grand slam home run.

13
Getting Down to Money

We assume naturally that you have not been so unwise as to include in your responses to advertising anything regarding your salary. In a cover letter you may make some passing reference to a general range which will interest you, but other than that, this group of strangers has no right to know what you make. They can offer all the threats they wish in the body of the ad; I have never yet seen a company turn down a qualified candidate for further inspection solely because he or she did not include the salary information demanded.

This means that, if you've acted properly, you will enter the company premises with neither of you having any idea of what the final salary figure is likely to be. In filling out the job application if there is one, you will dutifully note the salary desired box and write "open," as stated previously. When it comes to writing down former employers, you can give the salary data asked for, but relative to your current employer the situation will depend on your degree of desperation and how attractive the job seems to be. You can always wing it and put nothing, or, if you genuinely need this job, it may be best to comply with all their instructions.

Once you are actually interviewing, either with someone in personnel or the actual hiring manager, you will not broach the subject of salary, because that comes under the heading of "stupid moves", diluting your sales pitch and, for the moment, creating the ridiculous impression that you are the buyer before anybody has offered to sell you anything. Therefore, in this scenario, the first mention of money should come from the interviewer.

With respect to job applicants, I have learned that genuinely talented people who have legitimate reasons for finding a new employer but who, in the last analysis, could stay where they are will ordinarily be thinking in terms of a 15 to 25 percent increase in salary before they start getting interested. Those who are sufficiently unhappy in their current job that they are scanning the want ads daily and will take any interview offered may accept a lateral move but will usually try to use their leverage as an employed person to receive a ten percent increase. To those who are unemployed or know that their situation is grave enough for dismissal or layoff to be imminent, a lateral move will do, and many will accept up to a ten percent pay cut just to find a new position. Obviously these numbers are not carved in stone, but they represent the trends I have observed over the years talking to literally thousands of job candidates and tracking their success or failure in finding new employment.

On the company side there are two schools of thought, and I suspect the former is most prevalent. A company seeking to hire a professional-level employee will typically set a salary based on experience with other incumbents, any survey information they may have, or a general feel for the market. This salary "figure" can be as complex as a range calculated out to three decimal points, with grades and steps within grade (such as found in the federal government) or, usually in smaller companies, a general feeling on the part of executives concerned that some amount X is "about right." However, a lot of this goes out the window when they finally select a candidate and the ultimate question becomes, "What's the least we can get him for?" If they know your salary level and you don't have any idea of what they consider the job to be worth, you are clearly at a disadvantage.

In the second case, the companies will adhere to their research data and simply declare that anybody hired for a specific job will come in at the salary level called for.

Generally an occurrence in larger companies, I have seen this happen with remarkably happy results for the candidates. I recall one occasion where a Fortune 500 company was seeking a division personnel manager and had determined to pay a certain amount. They became enamored of an unusually young man and, upon learning of his relatively low salary, offered him what amounted to a 60 percent increase. Needless to say, he took it. I venture to say, however, that a smaller, less sophisticated company would have been moved to be generous, but not *that* generous. After all, even a 30 percent jump in pay is quite respectable, would doubtless have gotten him, and would have saved the firm a considerable sum.

Having offered a little philosophy on the subject, let me add that the profusion of executive recruiters in the United States today has narrowed these ranges considerably. At the risk of boasting, I think that we perform a valuable service to the market at large in making certain that companies pay market price for their professional talent. Years ago, it was common to find people such as the young man we spoke about being paid 10, 20, even 30 percent below market, even though they were doing an outstanding job. Such exploited individuals are pure gold for recruiters, because we can offer them immediate, sizable incentives to leave their niggardly employers and go elsewhere. I remember well how shocked people used to be when they discovered what their counterparts at other companies made, and I completed many assignments by taking such people from unappreciative employers and placing them with more enlightened ones. Companies today, though, increasingly aware of the existence of such "predators" as myself, have a simple choice as to the job market—they either pay an acceptable rate or lose a lot of good staff. All but the most obtuse choose the former.

It has gotten so that if I hear a person describe the last five years of their employment history for three minutes, I can guess their salary level and nine times out of ten come within 10 percent. To me, that validates the idea that the range of acceptable salaries for certain kinds of professional talent has narrowed considerably over the years.

This discussion of market forces and company attitutdes is not academic. It lays the groundwork for your strategy. In the absence of a third-party recruiter who will insure that you and the company are on the same dance floor before the first meeting, you are on your own and must deal with the salary question in such a way as neither to turn the firm away from you nor to sell yourself too cheaply. There are a variety of situations which you may confront. Let me show you the extremes.

A personnel officer may ask you in the screening interview how much you want. If your current situation is strong, you may be equally blunt and pleasantly observe that this isn't the time for such a discussion, since you've not even met the hiring manager yet. You run the risk that the personnel official may grunt, continue the interview for a short time with pursed lips, bid you good day, cast a few silent aspersions on your heritage, and toss your application in the circular file. You'll remember we dealt with the personnel department in Chapter 10.

Since we are assuming that this job is not for you a matter of life and death, this may be an acceptable risk, particularly when you consider that when other things are positive, personnel managers will not normally be so bold. There are a lot of ways to upset them, but being coy about salary is rarely one of them. After all, they know how the game is played, too.

If you are unemployed and the cupboard is bare, you may not wish to gamble but take the opposite tack, in which case your response will be that you need "something in the range of" and then insert two figures, the absolute minimum you can live on at the bottom and the salary you left at the top. Thus, if your most recent position paid $40,000 a year and you could not run your household on less than $30,000 your response would be "something in the range of $30 to $40,000." The tactic here is quite simply to sell yourself as cheaply as possible and, it is to be hoped, attract the company to the idea of getting a lot for a little, thereby making yourself more attractive than other candidates with similar skills but higher requirements. I should point out this works out best in smaller companies, where the salary policies are not too elaborate. If you're seeking to be hired by a large, sophisticated firm, you might modify this approach by stating a desire for something in the range of your last salary.

For situations that fall somewhere in the middle, I counsel more reticence than openness with personnel. Where you can afford to be rejected, it is better to be shot for a sheep than a lamb and if you are seeking a 25 percent salary increase to make a change, I would not let personnel know about it. It is always possible that you may not get passed to the hiring manager because the personnel manager doesn't like your attitude on the subject. If, on the other hand, they know your salary expectations and what you make now, you may be rejected for being " out of line," even though your talents merit the compensation you want. Personnel people are rarely as good a judge of market value in this regard as those at department level, and just because a hiring manager specifies a given salary level doesn't mean that he or she wouldn't cheerfully pay more, perhaps a lot more, for someone with unusual ability. You do not want the personnel officer making this decision for the hiring manager, hence my counsel about being tight-lipped if you can afford to do so.

Personnel people like to talk salary. It's their stock in trade, and they deal with it every day. Hiring managers will not typically discuss the subject until they become genuinely interested in your qualifications. At some point in the interview process, the gears will switch from evaluation to investigation; from "What can this person do?" to "What can he do for us?" From "Do I want him?" to "How can I get him?" Once that mental shift occurs, the hiring manager starts to think salary.

If you've answered an ad and told the personnel department what you want, the hiring manager knows what it will take to get you and salary negotiation is inconsequential. If you've been absolutely silent on the subject, the manager will, once the mental shift has taken place, probably ask what you have to have to go to work, or some other offhand kind of statement. It's interesting that everybody seems to approach the salary question, at least at the outset, in a cavalier way, as though it were an incidental item of only passing interest. If you have performed adequately in the interview and the hiring manager seems suitably impressed, you can be fairly straightforward. If you want to use the percentages outlined previously, go ahead. If you have some more ambitious figure in mind for increasing your current salary, that's all right too. I would, however, caution that if you're going to shoot for 50 percent or better, you had better have done one whale of a job in presenting astoundingly good credentials. Companies will sometimes offer such enormous advances to dumbfounded candidates because their corporate salary scales require it. If you go in asking for it, you may get a cooler reception than you bargained for. There is, after all, an element of appropriateness in these matters, and with annual increases for on-board employees running in the 7 to 10 percent range, you have to make an awfully good case to get 50 percent.

When your prospective boss first mentions the subject of salary, you can try one evasion and see if it works. For younger, relatively less experienced candidates, the comeback might be, "Well, I'm not exactly certain. I'm really more interested in a good opportunity. I expect you would be in the best position to know what my talents might be worth. Obviously, I'm looking for a long-term association and would want to be rewarded for what I contribute."

You haven't answered the question, but some people will bite and tell you what the job actually pays. Some won't, will dismiss your comment, and bore in again seeking to discover what you want to get paid. Since the etiquette of commerce dictates that the seller name his price unless the buyer demands to purchase something the owner really doesn't want to sell, you pretty much have to give a quantitative response at this point.

I've found over the years that the key tactic is to quote a range, starting at the least acceptable figure and, at the high end, stating an extremely attractive figure. The company has something to play with, and they have a decision to make. Since they don't know how desperately you want the job (and you have been responsive but not eager, I trust), they face risks at either extreme. If they cheerfully offer you the bottom number, the job may not be attractive enough and you will turn it down. If they offer you the top number, there's always that niggling worry that they could have gotten you for less, and who knows whether the news of your good fortune may get around the company, causing grumbling to start among those at peer level who are not so lavishly rewarded. If your bottom number is inside their range but the top number is outside it, you may still get a very nice offer. They may suggest a compromise that involves going two-thirds of the spread up from your bottom number, thus leaving you within their range and well above your least acceptable figure.

The other nice thing about quoting ranges is that it implies flexibility on your part. Many executives have told me that it just seems there's something cold and hard about a person who says "I want X dollars and that's that." Inflexibility is deemed a severe no-no in today's management circles, and you must take pains not to generate that impression in your prospective boss. Quoting a range relieves this difficulty and also gives the company a tough choice to chew on. Why not let them sweat a little?

I may as well let you in on a few secrets of our business here, in case your search for other employment involves using a third-party recruiter. We operate at many different levels and, most significantly, different levels of intimacy with the employer. At the top is a fully retained executive search in which the specifications are spelled out in a signed agreement and have been determined through a lengthy personal meeting between the recruiter and the company's board chairman. At the bottom is a contingency recruiter who has spent all of 30 seconds on the phone with a personnel officer whose face he has never seen, taking the barest possible facts about some position that has just become available and he happened to call at the right time. As you may appreciate, these assignments are worlds apart.

In the first case, with a retained search, you will almost invariably get solid, accurate data about what the company is willing to pay prior to your first meeting with a decision maker. You should respond by offering accurate information about what you make and what you expect. No respectable recruiter will proceed without it.

If the relationship is more tenuous, however, you have to be careful. Suppose the recruiter has indeed been talking to a voice at the personnel department of an unknown company seeking business and discovered that an opening does indeed exist. After the voice describes in no great detail what is wanted, the subject of pay eventually arises. Now, the personnel official knows that if this hitherto unknown agency comes up with the right candidate, the company will be obligated to pay a fee, usually ranging from 20 to 35 percent of the salary they agree to pay the candidate.

Perhaps this has not been budgeted for, so the personnel officer may try a ploy. If the job is actually worth $40,000, the recruiter may be told $30–$35,000, the hope being that if a talented person can be found for that kind of money, the difference between what they would have paid and what they got away with will help reduce the pain of paying the fee. This doesn't happen all the time, but it does happen sometimes, so you must be wary of revealing your earnings to contingency recruiters.

Remember, too, that employment agency counselors (as they are called) are savvy about these things, and will be delighted to present a quality candidate for $30,000 even if they can go as high as $40,000. They reason that the less expensive a good candidate is, the more likely it is that they can place him with a company glad to get real talent at a cheap price and willing to pay the fee without a fuss. I know of one agency in my own city that has built a rather sizable business by convincing more or less desperate people to take large salary cuts and join their client firms, who are only too happy to get them below market price. The kicker is, or course, that if another recruiter comes along and tells them what they're actually worth, they may easily be induced to leave that employer for yet another one; then the hapless client company goes back to these same good folks for another bargain basement special. Some companies do not learn.

So I've said, tell the recruiter everything about your earnings, and also tell him nothing. You may ask yourself, "What kind of sense does that make?" How do you know which advice to take when?

It is easy to discover which response to use. If you are contacted by a recruiter, ask them, "Are you on a retained assignment?" If they say yes, they will either be lying to impress you or telling the truth, but if they're lying it's not hard to uncover. Any fully retained recruiter worthy of the name has a thorough understanding of what his or her assignment calls for. Naturally they will not reveal the identity of their clients, but they can tell you other things which will make it abundantly clear that they have had meetings with senior management and know the specifications cold. They can tell you the approximate size of the firm, the number of employees, the title of the person to whom the job reports, the number of people supervised, some of the major areas of responsibility, certain financial data couched in terms that will be relevant if you are invited for interview and useless if you're not, the level of EDP support, the reason the position is available, and a host of other things that simply are not said to strangers in two-minute phone calls.

Contingency recruiters don't usually even bother getting such details, even if they could. The reason is that they handle a large number of "job orders" in the hope of filling a small fraction of them. This approach does not allow the luxury of spending much time gathering data from any one company. It is essentially a volume business that succeeds on the basis of percentages.

It is possible, though thank heaven not too probable, that your friendly recruiter may be the hopelessly devious sort who guesses at answers to your questions, or even manufactures facts just to keep you talking. All I can say is, write down what he or she says and, at the first clear evidence of fabrication, *cease your dealings with that person immediately*. If the recruiter can give you substantive answers, you give quantitative answers about your compensation. If he gives you generalities, or responds "I don't know" several times instead of answers, you must be coy. If he asks what you make, you ask what they're offering. If it sounds like an unusually attractive position and you'd like to pursue it, but are by no means desperate, you might quote your expectations at 25 percent above what you make now and see what happens. Who knows, you could even latch onto something good.

Leaving the subject of recruiters, let's return to how you go about determining what these people will pay. Keeping in mind that your degree of inquisitiveness is always inversely proportional to your desperation, you can always ask what the previous incumbent was making. If that's a nice-sounding number, you can make a very good case for getting no less than that, since the person they're replacing couldn't do the job and they're hiring you on the assumption that you can. If it's not such a nice number, you simply disregard it and use the other ideas presented above to develop your negotiating posture.

Many jobs today, particularly at senior levels, have a percentage of the compensation based upon incentive—money that you get only by performing well. I am always amazed at how airily these things are dismissed by hiring managers, sometimes senior executives in the companies I've represented, as though "All that can be worked out later." If you seek a position where a significant portion of your earnings will be based upon incentive, this is a place where you just have to get tough. If they don't like it, you can pretty well rest assured that the incentive was more promise than substance.

I still shake my head thinking of the number of people who have talked with me about changing employers because a verbal agreement was not honored, and the candidates sadly realized that their employers had been lying to them all along. You are well advised to stay out of this trap by getting very specific regarding bonuses and other programs the company says will be included as part of your package.

The first thing to discuss is criteria—the standards upon which incentive compensation will be based. If the job you seek is largely oriented toward production, the standard is likely to be based on sales volume, or revenue generated. But that's not enough. You need to know the specifics, the break points, the percentages, a schedule of what fraction of given dollar volumes will come to you as the producer of that volume. Is there a specific formula, or is the bonus discretionary based upon hitting some target to qualify? I urge that you must not let them off the hook by accepting generalized statements. If they get upset at your probing, that's just too bad. At this point in the process you have a legitimate right to know, and you should pursue the knowledge in defense of your own career interests.

Another thing you'll want to know is how often bonuses are paid. Annual bonuses are nice, but you can't really live on them. If you have a $60,000 salary with a $20,000 bonus paid in December, you cannot comfortably develop an $80,000 standard of living. You can, of course, salt away the bonus and withdraw a portion every month to supplement your regular pay, but that presupposes it will always be there. If you live to the limit of your income and the bonus disappears one year, you could be in big trouble.

Conversely, a quarterly or even monthly cash incentive can more easily be regarded as regular income and used to enhance your standard of living.

Frequently, however, there will be no formula at all, and the company will offer something called a *discretionary bonus* based upon performance. This can involve a certain amount of evaluation by your new superiors in a genuine effort to come up with a figure that reflects your true value to the company, or it may be dependent upon what the chairman of the board has for breakfast on the morning he decides to give out bonuses. It is a matter of no small interest that you determine just how "discretionary" a discretionary bonus will be.

The difficulty is that, when you ask how the bonus will be structured, you may get a response like, "That's hard to say, Pat, because there are so many variables to consider. We expect you to participate in a lot of new ventures next year, and we don't know how each one will pan out. That's why we can't put together a formula the way we'd like. There's just no way to know what the numbers will be."

That sounds reasonable, but it doesn't get you anywhere. There is a way, though, to penetrate this fog and either make the company give you some concrete information or satisfy yourself that what they're promising doesn't exist anywhere except inside their heads.

Many companies in these situations say they want to be generous. You first need to pin down what the word "generous" means to them. By looking at the job they are offering, you can use what you know about it to approach them this way:

"George, let me ask you something. If I join your company here and perform in accordance with the game plan you've outlined, what could I expect in the way of a bonus based upon what you know about me?"

If George hems and haws, you need to prod him a bit—you need to suggest a figure, either in dollars or a percentage of salary, that might be right. You need to get him to say something that has a number in it, or you've got nothing to evaluate.

In circumstances where the job involves bringing business into the firm, the bonus will normally be a percentage of that revenue. Here again, the hiring manager may express a desire to be generous, in which case your question is, "What is your definition of generous?" To some people, one percent of revenue is generous, but to others it's five percent. If you consider generous to be $100,000, you'd better make sure the hiring manager doesn't think generous means $10,000. You see why it's just plain necessary to be specific *before* you accept the job?

But again, you may get the old soft shoe; something to the

effect that it's just too hard to tell. Your final attempt to elicit useful facts should focus on history. You should ask, quite frankly, assuring the hiring manager that you don't want any names bandied about, what others in the firm get in the way of bonuses—what your peers received last year. Assure your prospective boss that you don't want to know who got what, just the kinds of dollars or percentages that were involved. If real bonuses exist, he should have no trouble responding:

"All right. One of our people in acquisitions makes something over $100,000 and last year she brought in a major deal, so we gave her $25,000 to show our appreciation. A fellow in marketing usually produces $2 million a year and gets 2 percent of volume on top of a salary that's regarded as 5 to 10 percent better than others in our industry. We take care of our people."

This is not telling stories out of school; you don't know who these folks are, and you're not going to use this information against the firm. You have, however, obtained a substantial indicator of how management values its key employees. With a few more examples provided by your prospective boss, you follow with:

"Could I expect to be rewarded in similar fashion in this position we're talking about if I perform well, too?"

Now, you see, the manager has got to give you an answer. If he says no, you ask why not. If he says yes, you've at long last learned something genuinely pertinent to your negotiation.

Not every company is cagey, and not every one is devious. I'm glad to say that most are run by people of good will who, when they make a job offer, want the new employee to be happy. However, sad as I am to say it, there simply are instances where, because they want you badly, they will lead you to believe things about the opportunity that are just not true. Remember, it only has to happen to you once to make an indelible mark on your career. The questioning sequence above should not offend any honorable person seeking to make a major job offer. If none of these tactics produce numbers that mean something, you need to be very careful indeed.

In cases where the bonus arrangement is completely discretionary or has few objective elements, you can try for a bonus guarantee, in which both parties stipulate that, regardless of the company's fortunes, some percentage of the "target bonus" will definitely be forthcoming provided that your work is sufficiently satisfactory and that you remain in the company's employ for a full year. This protects you somewhat from the arbitrary nature of discretionary bonuses and is a measure of good faith on the company's part. Without objective criteria or a guarantee, you will have to trust your prospective boss a great deal. Many times these arrangements do work out; many times they don't.

Some companies offer bonus programs that they haven't developed yet; then they actually do develop them and handsomely reward those who trusted them. Some top managers have truly generous spirits and regularly hand out bonuses that would blow your mind—you should only be so fortunate—and nothing about them is either written or promised anywhere. They expect you to trust them. (That's where getting some real but anonymous history will help a lot.)

Just remember human nature. How much do you want to place an important aspect of your life in the hands of a total stranger? Remember what I said earlier, you only really know a person when you have trouble with him. My experience is that, for every open-hearted, generous CEO, there are several who will promise the world until it comes time to pay. Consider the possibility that what you can't get up front may never be paid outside of a lawsuit, and who needs that! As those of experience in these matters say, "Get it going in!"

There's the usual smorgasbord of benefits, and you should pleasantly but firmly bring them into the open for discussion. Is there a company car provided, or an automobile allowance? What kind of insurance program do they offer, and does the company pay all premiums or does the employee have to contribute to some extent? If you are relocating, you need a complete description of the package, including house-hunting trips, moving expenses, payment of the real estate commission to sell your current home, and—if the economy gets like that again—mortgage differential. What about equity or stock options? Does the firm have a profit sharing or pension plan? These things are rather obvious, and this is just sort of a checklist to make sure you don't miss anything.

Then, too, there's the subject of the title you will receive if the job is at corporate officer level. Here again, some companies, particularly smaller ones, like to stay loose on this matter, shrugging it off as though titles don't matter. They *do* matter, particularly if you expect to have peers whom you may have to battle for a choice promotion. Senior vice-presidents have an edge on vice-presidents, and I don't care who says it doesn't mean anything. Don't arrive for work and find out the title you had in mind was not the one they had in mind.

One of the most frequently asked questions is whether or not someone about to be offered a job should require a contract. Quite frankly, there are various schools of thought on this subject, and I offer my view as one of many which could have merit. This is relatively deep water, and you will need to judge each situation for yourself.

I counsel that only two types of individuals should seek contracts: one, those who are securely employed, are under no immediate pressure to leave, and are being courted by a firm that wants them desperately and two, those whose performance has such a powerful effect upon the company's fortunes that they can be called a bottom-line decision maker. Typically only three roles fulfill this requirement, those being chief executive officer, chief operating officer, and executive vice-president. In a small company those will be the top three people, period. In larger ones it would be the positions corresponding to those in operating units, subsidiaries, or divisions. Obviously, group vice-presidents or members of senior corporate staff in a multilayered large company would also be included.

The trouble with contracts is that employers know they are hopelessly one-sided. Employees can break them with little difficulty, because the jobs people do at these levels require dedication and creativity, two things which cannot be forced out of people at legal gunpoint. Conversely, the employer is bound by the terms of the contract to provide money or other compensation in case the business marriage goes awry. For this reason, companies don't like to offer contracts and, I have found, are none too happy when lower-level employees request them.

A contract is simply a legally enforceable document which sets forth all the things you and your prospective employer agreed you should have in order to go to work for them. It discusses salary level, lots of detail on the bonus arrangements, benefits, other perquisites such as company car or country club memberships and, on the other side, declares that you will serve them faithfully to the very best of your ability. The only unique feature is that it specifies a time limit. This is usually one or two years, sometimes three, rarely five unless the job in question is CEO of a large company. If the employer reneges on the deal, you can enforce the contract in court, perhaps to the extent of receiving the entire amount of your agreed-upon compensation for the balance of its term. If you break the deal, the company can seek legal remedies, but I have rarely seen one do so, except in the case of noncompete clauses, which have been successfully used against those seeking to leave their employer to join a competitor. A noncompete clause makes such a move illegal, and courts will enforce these clauses.

One executive, whom I successfully enticed away from a major national corporation to be senior vice-president of operations for a smaller one, had the most carefully worded, legally sound, bluntly threatening contract I had ever seen. He was of immense value to his existing employer and, when they learned he was about to take another job, threatened him with all manner of things. They threatened the chairman of the new company; attorneys for both sides became involved, and many letters went back and forth over several weeks, to say nothing of numerous phone calls. But, in the end, the man was released by his existing employer because they knew he would be no good to them held there by a chain rather than love of his job. That's why employers don't like contracts.

If you're going to require a contract, get a good one. Make sure it's legally enforceable by consulting an attorney who will insure that all the legal niceties are there. At the outset everyone is all smiles and handshakes, but, if divorce appears to be looming, all parties will scurry for copies of the actual writing and begin plotting strategy based on interpretation of the words themselves. Be protected up front, and you'll have less of a fight on your hands at the end if you have to enforce the provisions of the agreement.

The thing companies don't like about contracts, in addition to the difficulty of enforcing the employee's end of the agreement, is the time limit. When a two-year contract calls for not less than $150,000 salary plus bonuses and perquisites and then the employee lasts only six months, because of personality factors or something else which nobody foresaw, the firm will frequently balk at the prospect of paying the person 18 months' compensation for doing nothing. These cases frequently wind up in court, and the only real winners are the lawyers. The executive may get his money, but he will never be able to use the firm as a reference, and they may indeed be able to hurt him behind his back. The company may pay dearly for nothing and have a most bitter taste in their mouths, which will be remembered when someone else comes along wanting a contract.

A much more frequently obtainable concept is the termination agreement. Even middle managers get these without too much difficulty, and they are very similar to contracts except for their duration. Essentially, the candidate and employer agree that, should involuntary termination be necessary through no fault of the new employee, the company will provide certain things. Those are typically a larger than usual severance pay, continuation of group insurance, perhaps use of a company vehicle until a new position is secured plus a variety of other possibilities. While companies may usually give two weeks' severance for new employees who must be let go, the termination agreement may call for three months' severance and benefits. In some cases, with higher-level employees or a riskier company situation, the agreement may be a six-month arrangement. I have even seen them as long as one year, which is about the length of the shortest formal contract generally found. Here again, as with so many aspects of this kind of negotiation, the key features are the company's eagerness to get you and your relative degree of desperation to leave your current firm.

It's never pleasant to discuss divorce while you're making wedding plans, but these issues must be faced. True marriage is supposed to be for life; business marriages seldom are. This is not Japan. If you don't face the possibility that the new job may not work out, you may discover to your sorrow that the company has a bad quarter, you are no longer necessary, and you get a check for two weeks' pay and a pat on the back. If you left a position which you had for five years and were employed by these new people for five months, that is a bitter pill indeed. Such things happen more frequently than you might suppose. If you can get a termination agreement, my advice is to press for it, particularly if you're gainfully employed and in no immediate danger of losing your job.

Even if you have neither contract nor termination agreement, you should definitely get your offer in writing. This is the very least the company can do, and if they are unwilling to send you a letter detailing your title, salary, bonus (if any), and any special benefits or perquisites which you both may have agreed to, my judgment is that you are not dealing with honorable people. I fear that those who refuse such a simple request have something to hide. The letter, sent to your home, simply declares a mutual understanding which hopefully has been the desired result of your negotiation all along. My counsel is that you should not approach your current employer on the subject of your resignation until you have such a letter in hand.

Having that written communication from your prospective employer sitting in your bureau drawer at home is good emotional backup for your confrontation with those you must tell goodbye. More on that in Chapter 15.

14
Now That They Are Yours

You have reached the exhilarating moment, that moment when you receive a telephone call from somebody representing a firm which you believe you would like to join offering you the position for which you have been interviewing. Being chosen is always a heady experience, but it's at this time that you must be even more alert than previously. The reason is that your emotions may betray you into accepting the job without doing some careful thinking and asking some questions of your own. The thinking and asking must come before the acceptance, or else you may find yourself in a muddle that may be worse than the employer you left.

Sometimes the offer will come in the call itself and all the details will be spelled out—salary, benefits, starting date, where you should report, and other similar information. For lower-level positions this is standard, and invariably the companies expect an immediate acceptance so they can get about doing other things. If you give it to them, you will have no turn "at bat" and will be walking into a situation that is, notwithstanding the questions you may have asked previously, largely unknown to you.

Business corporations are, by their nature, self-interested organizations. They will not typically look out for anyone else's welfare but their own unless forced to do so. If you accept a job on the basis of information given and received at face value while they were evaluating you, no member of the personnel department or the group you will be joining is likely to present you with a series of caveats about the company's financial condition, the character of management, or anything else that might be useful in determining what you are really getting into. If they get your acceptance, as far as they're concerned, that's the end of it. If, three months later, you discover to your horror that the place is a total can of worms and you had no idea it was going to be like that and you are jolly well going to quit, the company will not grieve for very long. They will simply go out and hire somebody else, and perhaps throw in a less than glowing reference about you if someone should ask. The only real loser will be you.

There are some companies that are absolute revolving doors when it comes to the professional positions they must fill to stay in business. Company representatives do not make a habit of informing prospective employees of this fact, since all that will do is make their jobs harder in the interim period while they themselves are looking for something else.

Not every company is short-sighted and self-centered, but I venture to say that there are more than you realize. If you accept a job with one of them, their problems become your own. They are problems you don't need.

Considering for the moment positions below senior management, you can perhaps ask your questions and get some satisfactory answers over the phone, particularly if the call has come from the hiring manager directly rather than personnel. Here is where you and the employer finally exchange hats, as it were; you become the buyer and he or she must do the selling. Your personal agenda, not the company's, is now the topic at hand. Companies do not like to be put in this position but, if you have been prudent up to now, your future boss will, we hope, take it in reasonably good grace. After all, he knows that you have needs and desires too and, if he has any understanding of human nature, will expect that the subject of your personal career needs must come up sooner or later. This will be no surprise to a good manager and, if it is, you have your first red flag.

At this point the matter of your own eagerness deserves consideration. If you've been out of work for six months and the contents of the refrigerator are a bit skimpy, it is wise not to be too difficult to please. You never know what may turn a hiring manager off. This aspect of these negotiations is quite simply a mine field and if you step on a mine, you've blown the offer. You don't know what will irritate the manager—what kind of question, what sort of innuendo—and furthermore you don't know whether he has a number two or even a number three candidate in mind who is nearly as good as you. Here again, the key is the character, personality, and ego drive of the person with whom you're dealing. By asking even a few probing questions of a prickly hiring manager who has another good candidate in his pocket, you could find that an initially pleasant call turns very chilly. He might even say that something has come up, and he'll get back to you, and that's the last you hear. Call the company back, and you then get the usual mumblings about the company having decided to "do something else." You could go to the government and complain about this treatment and might even win your case, but the best thing is to not let it happen at all.

Making the other assumption, you may be in the happy situation where you are currently employed by a reasonably good company, but this offer is for more money with more responsibility, so it looks very attractive. Coupled with this, three other recruiters have called you in the last month and, wonder of wonders, you are so sought after that you have two other offers pending. Let us further assume that there is nobody except those with whom you have interviewed who has the slightest idea that you are exploring other opportunities. In this pleasant circumstance, you are totally in the driver's seat, and you can make yourself as difficult as you wish with the personnel department, the hiring manager, or even the president of the interested company because if they don't do exactly as you wish, you can bid them good day, having lost nothing. I have selected these two extremes to show you the nature of the continuum. Clearly the tricky part is when your situation is somewhere in the middle.

To further belabor the eagerness factor, consider that it consists of several parameters. If you are unemployed, the main points are how long you've been out of work, the condition of your finances, and whether you have any other good prospects. If you are employed, you must look at the financial condition of your company, the direction of the political winds inside the firm and how they may affect your own career there, and whether you are being appreciated in both emotional and financial terms by your superiors. The third parameter relates to the company and the position being offered. How attractive is it compared to what you have now, again expressed in terms of compensation, political or emotional factors, and the overall prospects for the company?

It all sounds very nice when laid out this way, but the trouble comes when you are attempting to mix these ingredients together to form a decision. Money will play a role; emotional factors will play a role; the relative sizes and strengths of the companies will play a role; how much you like your prospective boss or dislike your old one will be important; your prospects for advancement must be considered, and, interestingly, you too may experience that metaphysical rush about which we spoke earlier in those cases where everything seems to be coming together just perfectly. The trouble is that none of these factors have numbers assigned to them, so you can't really be sure you're making a good move; you can only take the available information and do your best with it. The key is to get as much relevant information as possible without losing so much political capital that even if you do take the job, there will be ill feelings among those who know how deeply you probed before you accepted the offer.

If you think this is all too arcane, too involved, too Machiavellian to be real, let me assure you it's not. I suggest that people who don't believe that these things are relevant simply have little or no exposure to the process. I have seen numerous instances where companies developed "attitudes" against very attractive job candidates because they wanted certain kinds of information to help them decide about making a move. Many professional men and women regard their careers as the most important thing in their lives and that, coupled with the intense ego involvement with their companies that such people often exhibit, makes for an explosive mix when strangers come around asking tough questions. In my years as a recruiter I have seen repeatedly that it does not take much in the way of improper comment or poorly phrased questions to drop the temperature in a room twenty degrees. It seems to me that people these days are a bit more thin-skinned than they used to be, so, even though the company is selling and you are buying, you must still be extremely diplomatic in the process.

Having set the stage and, I hope, given you the flavor of this type of negotiation, let us move to a scene in which you are attempting to evaluate a pretty good job at the middle management level in a situation where you essentially have most of the cards. You can be as tough as you want and still not be hurt (unless you get crude and the company retaliates by advising your current employer of your extracurricular activities), but you still would like to have the job if it's as good as it looks. What you need now is solid information to help you decide.

At this point I must stress the value of your discussing these important things with the hiring manager in person. If it's at all possible, you should, after expressing warm appreciation for having been chosen, request another meeting with your prospective boss to explore some issues that have not been adequately covered. This is something of an imposition, of course, but if you have played your cards properly up to now and the hiring manager really wants you, you will get the meeting. It is a whole lot easier to handle these discussions face to face rather than over the phone, primarily because you can view the facial expressions that result from your asking certain types of questions. Some managers naturally play very good poker, but others are quite expressive, and when the topic is company weaknesses you can learn a lot by watching closely as your prospective boss reacts to what you really want to know.

If the position involves relocation from a substantial distance, the follow-up meeting to discuss your agenda is much more difficult to arrange unless you want to pay for the trip yourself, which most people prefer not to do. Asking the company to foot the bill for airfare and lodging so that you can ask them questions is, in my judgment, not a wise use of political capital. In this circumstance, you will almost certainly have to get what you need over the phone. Don't worry about the company's burning their nickels in a long conversation; remember, they want to hire you and understand that this is part of the process.

Another thing to think about is that, if you are facing a significant relocation, some of the questions which follow may be asked during the initial interview trip to the company location, preferably toward the end of the visit, if you feel that things have been going well. You will, of course, have to judge which questions are innocuous enough to be included before they have made up their mind about you and which are so sensitive that they must wait until afterward. In the following discussion of subjects to address, we will begin with those that I consider easy and move on toward the tougher ones. These can be asked over the phone or in person but, as I said, in person is invariably better.

The first thing you want to know about is the history of this particular job. Is it new? Has it been filled before? How many incumbents have there been in the last ten years? Why did they leave? If they were dismissed, what was it about their performance that was unsatisfactory? If they resigned, did they give any indication as to why? What can the hiring manager tell you about the relative strengths and weaknesses of the previous incumbents?

That's just a smorgasbord, but you get the idea. If the job is new and there has never been an incumbent in it, you have your second red flag. This opens up a whole new line of questioning, and it is extremely relevant to you. Consider that the company has operated with presumed success for X number of years without this job's having been in existence. What is to say that six months from now they may not decide the position is superfluous, along with you? As I said, most companies are self-centered to the core, and your survival in such a situation is highly doubtful. It is simply not common for companies to take persons of average talent and find other spots for them if the have been employed for short periods. This does happen on occasion, but usually with individuals whose intelligence and abilities are so obviously superior that everyone in the company can recognize that fact in a few months. Unless you have an extraordinary track record with previous employers, the prospect of taking a newly created job must be viewed warily.

In this context, the line of questioning might run as follows: How was it decided to create this position? Who participated in the decision, or who actually made it? What is happening inside the firm to make this job necessary at this time? What has the company been doing about this function until now? What sort of budget has been allocated?

Again, there are myriads of additional questions that can branch off from these main topics I have presented. The idea here is to show you how to open the company up and see what's inside there before making a critical decision. For example, if your position has been authorized by the chairman of the board because the company has decided to enter a new line of business, and the firm has committed significant funding to the project, and the future success of the company will depend largely upon the success of this venture, you are in pretty good shape. At the other extreme, if the position was created by the hiring manager himself to solve a particular problem that may be short-term in nature and he has given very little thought to the subject of budget, red flags should be flying all over the place. If you don't ask, you won't find out until you're aboard. Then, if the revelation is unpleasant, you're stuck.

You may be thinking that companies just don't hire people for supposedly full-time positions where the goals are short-term and they really haven't any idea of what to do with you afterward. Don't bet on it! I have seen it happen scores of times, though fortunately have participated in very few such assignments. Companies will, in all too many cases, deceive a prospective employee in order to reach whatever objectives they feel are necessary for success. I stress that not all firms are like this, but there are an appreciable number. Unless you are interviewing General Motors or Exxon Corporation or some other household name, it is wisest to assume that you will need everything you can learn to make a smart decision. I have even known some large, highly visible companies to pull a few fast ones on sought-after job candidates, so may I take this opportunity to scream at you, *"Caveat emptor!"* or *"Let the buyer beware!"* Obviously this goes for both you and the company, but if it doesn't work out, you will be hurt far more severely than they unless you are seeking a corporate-officer position, which is a whole different ball game and will be discussed later on.

If the job is a line position, standard in every company, such as controller, sales manager, or customer service representative and if it has been around for years and will be around for years more, you need to focus on previous incumbents, as suggested earlier. I don't recommend your asking how many incumbents there were in the last ten years—that's a bit too tacky. I suggest beginning with the last one or, in a highly confidential situation, the current one, and asking how long he or she has or had been employed. Then go on to the points brought up previously—strengths and weaknesses, reasons for leaving, and so on. Once you have a pretty good feel for what that individual's experience was like, you can move to the previous incumbent, then the one prior to that, until you've covered an adequate span of time.

If the incumbent has been in the job five years and is retiring, you have a reasonably secure situation. By finding out what the company liked about that person, discerning some personal factors, you will have a good idea of what the firm is likely to expect from you. On the other hand, if the present incumbent is being fired and doesn't know it yet after having been on the job six months, and the previous incumbent had the job six months and the previous incumbent had the job six months, bells should be going off inside your head about once every second. At this point you have nothing to lose by grilling the hiring manager thoroughly to find out why nobody could satisfy him, what his true expectations are and, if you really want to get blunt, why he thinks you will do any better. Unless his answers are awfully good or your refrigerator is totally empty, my advice is that you pleasantly thank him for the offer and pass. The likelihood of such an arrangement working out is almost nil, and why should you saddle yourself with a period of short-term employment that must be explained to the next company you interview with?

I find most people are remarkably ignorant about how frequently new hiring situations fizzle after just a few months. Having been in this business for as long as I have, let me say that the frequency is much higher than one might suppose. It seems to me that years ago companies and employees both tried to make the best of things when they weren't ideal. Nowadays, though, the situation is more often remedied by swift dismissal. I have seen cases where new top management will come into a company and literally wipe out the second and third tiers in order to establish control and replace those managers with people loyal to them. It is genuinely a different ball game today, and the risks to you as a job candidate and prospective employee are far greater than they used to be. It's wise for you to acknowledge this fact and keep your guard up until such time as you actually accept a position.

Let us assume that the job is reasonably secure or that previous incumbents have had reasonably happy tenure and therefore this place on the organizational chart looks good. The next subject to address is the hiring manager himself or herself.

Here is the sequence that most likely might have been brought up prior to the offer being made, although it will most likely have been done in an incidental manner. After the business portion of the interview was over, perhaps a little chitchat ensued in which the hiring manager decided to tell you about himself. This is nice, but rarely does it go deep enough. On the assumption, however, that you do not have any real information to go on, the following topics should be addressed:

How long has he been with the firm? How long has he been in this particular job? Why does he think he was selected for his job? What company did he come from? How long was he there and in what position? How did he happen to come in contact with this current firm? Why did he decide to take the job? On the whole, does he feel it has worked out for him well? What does he think are the most outstanding characteristics of the company? What are its most significant weaknesses? What's the biggest challenge he's had to face in the job he holds now? What does he expect from a subordinate in the way of communication? What does he consider a reasonable timetable in which the person hired for this job should show some real progress? How would he describe his management style? How would he describe his philosophy of business? What does he think of the company's position with respect to its competitors, and upon what does he base that opinion? How does he react when things don't go just right? What sort of disciplinary system does he use with his employees? What kind of standard does he use to evaluate employee performance?

I hope you get the picture. You may think that I'm stressing these questions overmuch, as though learning all of this seems to be finding out things you don't really need or want to know. Although it's true that ignorance is sometimes bliss, it's also true that many times ignorance can lead into a situation that is totally untenable.

People who do not spend their lives around the ebb and flow of personalities inside business corporations have little conception of the extent to which those changes at all levels impact the success and growth or problems and decline experienced by companies large and small. The essence of corporate culture and, unfortunately, corporate politics, revolves around the players inside the companies. For purposes of making an important career decision, the characteristics in which you must be most interested are motives and integrity. If those are all right, you can probably get along with a loud back slapper or a prickly recluse, because no organization is composed of perfect people. But if the company is owned by a tyrant or has a reputation for instability or has managers at all levels who crack the whip and never offer praise, you don't want to be associated with it. Again, at the risk of boring you, I suggest that it is better to find this out in advance rather than after you have severed ties with your current company and have no choice but to make the best of it or start looking for work again.

Some of the trickiest information to get concerns the character and abilities of the chief executive officer or CEO—the man or woman who actually makes the final decisions and runs the company. This is critical if the job you seek has any significant level of authority and it can even have some impact on more modest positions that rarely interact with the chief executive but are nevertheless influenced by his policies. In most business corporations, particularly small ones, the character and personality of the CEO are reflected downward throughout all levels of management, and the company itself tends to take on those characteristics. There are, of course, exceptions, but the validity of this statement applies across a remarkably broad spectrum of industries, company sizes, and organizational structures. It does not matter that your prospective boss is a really great guy or gal if the one who runs or even owns the company is a hard-eyed, devious skinflint who uses people like a carpenter uses nails. That fact is going to have an impact upon your employment with the firm no matter at what level you join. Particularly in small organizations, the traits of the president will filter down throughout the ranks of his subordinates until the character of the company begins to resemble his own. A person who doesn't "fit in" with his approach to business, attitude toward people, and general philosophy of life may wind up as a short-term employee. That might well be you, or perhaps that pleasant prospective boss of yours.

Some questions you might address to your prospective boss about the CEO could include the following: How long has he been with the company? If he's not the owner and his tenure is less than two years, why was he brought into the firm? What are the most significant changes he's made since becoming CEO? Did he hire the prospective boss? If yes, what thoughts does the boss have about why he was hired? If you didn't get to meet the CEO yourself, what kind of person is he? Has there been a lot of turnover in the firm since he became CEO? What's his greatest strength, his greatest weakness, his greatest accomplishment, his greatest failure? Where was he before this company? Did he come up the marketing, finance, or operations track? What kind of management style does he exhibit with his immediate subordinates? What sort of temperament does he display when things go wrong? Has he fired a lot of his senior staff since becoming CEO?

This is just a starter kit to point you in the right direction. There are obviously many other questions that can be asked so that you can find out something about the character of the person who controls the company and, if you join it, your day-to-day working life.

In dealing with questions about senior management, I must stress the need for a diplomatic approach, particularly if your career has not yet reached the policy-making level. Corporate officers seeking to join the firm can and should get downright picky about this person's character, because it will have a powerful influence upon their daily activities. Lower-level people need to use more of an offhand, "by the way" type of approach and not bore in too heavily unless something seems terribly amiss in some of the answers. The fact is that your prospective boss should know the answers to most of these questions. If, when you ask for value judgments about the CEO's personality, style, and attitude toward people, he becomes skittish and evasive, then there could be real problems ahead. If, on the other hand, the company is truly a good place to work and the hiring manager is a real professional, you will get good, solid answers and even score points with your careful, logical approach to a major decision. People with nothing to hide don't hide things, and they appreciate the opportunity to be forthright. Nevertheless, it is up to you to find out; nobody offers this kind of information voluntarily.

We should direct a little additional emphasis to one of the previous questions in conjunction with another. If your prospective boss was not hired at the instigation of the current president, who has been with the firm for a short period of time, watch out. You need to ask how many people this relatively new CEO has replaced, and at what levels. It may be that the person you hope to work for is not slated to be aboard much longer. In that event, you could face the situation where you resign your current position, take the new job, lose the boss you wanted to work for, and get a new one about whom you know nothing. At best, this produces anxiety. At worst, your new boss may decide he wants a loyal team member and that, because you were hired by a previous manager, you don't qualify. Calamity may result.

The last thing of importance is the condition of the company. This not only encompasses financial status, but also its position in the market, the progress of new ventures, any problems it may be encountering with a significant line of business, and any news regarding the company or industry which may have significant impact upon the firm's future. Obviously, it doesn't matter that everyone in the place is wonderful if the firm is about to declare Chapter 11 next week. I stress again that not all companies are truthful about these things, and you had best ferret out the information before you get a nasty surprise. If you have the time and access, I suggest a trip to the morgue of the local newspaper, where you can browse through articles that may have been written about the company. If the firm is public, you naturally will read its 10-K (the official document required by the SEC which discloses every significant fact about its business and financial condition), forgetting the eyewash known as an annual report. Interim financial statements should also be part of your investigation.

If you can discover through these means that at this moment the company's future is reasonably bright, that is really all you need. If negative articles have appeared in the local press, you may have to ask what the company did to address the problem of "whatever it is" and what the status is now. Watch for waffling or an excessive degree of generality in the response. If your current employment situation offers you the luxury, don't be afraid to press. After all, it's your life on the line. I say it's better in that case to lose an offer because you asked some tough questions and they got huffy than to be excessively nice and discover you've landed in a can of worms. Remember, you only get one turn at bat, so make it a good one.

To sum up, it is fair to say that a financially stable company with a competent and honorable president will be a pretty good place to work. Further, if the hiring manager is also competent and honorable and has been with the firm for a fairly good length of time, holding his current position long enough to know what he's doing, you may conclude that you've been offered a good job if everything checks out with your goals. This, of course, involves the relative attractiveness of what you're being offered versus what you're leaving behind.

There is a particular type of additional emphasis necessary when the position you've been offered reports to the chief operating officer or higher level within a self-contained firm, corporate group, or headquarters situation. If you will be reporting to the individual who has either complete or a certain amount of profit and loss responsibility at any of these levels, the politics get a good deal thicker, and you need to ask some questions that those at lower levels needn't bother with.

Again, these things are dictated by your personal circumstances, but if you have any luxury at all in terms of turning the job down without serious harm to yourself, you should insist upon a meeting in person with the particular individual who holds authority for that unit, group or, in the case of extremely high-level positions, entire corporate structure. It is unlikely that you will get the kind of quality information you need from any other source.

If you are being offered the executive vice-presidency of a twenty-million-dollar division of a $5 billion conglomerate, it is unlikely that you'll get a meeting with the chairman of the board. You can and should, however, seek a meeting with the vice-president/general manager, even if that's not the person you would report to. If your prospective boss becomes miffed, that in itself may be a red flag. If it's impossible to get the meeting in person, at least try for 20 uninterrupted minutes on the telephone with him or her, because there are some very critical issues you need to discuss. Better 20 minutes on the phone with the right person than a face-to-face talk with someone who's not in a position to tell you anything useful.

The right kind of company will not balk. Intelligent business people know, because they have to make these decisions for their own careers, that a senior-level executive needs to be not only well compensated but also challenged and reasonably politically secure in order to do an optimum job. In most companies, there is an enormous amount of time and energy wasted on corporate politics which could be used to further the goals of the organization. The amount of infighting, assassination by deadly memo, covering up of mistakes, and procrastination is truly extraordinary, and one has to be in a position like mine to see how widespread it is. Most people see the inner workings of perhaps ten companies throughout their career; I see hundreds, both thorugh the eyes of incumbent management and those who have left, either in disgust or disgrace.

I estimate that 60 to 70 percent of the corporate leavetakings, whether it's the company or the executive initiating, are due largely to politics. Most of the casualties are losers in the rather endless battle for position and power within the corporate structure, and frequently when I contact somebody about another opportunity and find a receptive ear, the reason will be that the individual perceives the tide going against him or her.

For this reason, you need to know the lay of the land before you join the battle. A smart CEO will not object to this and indeed may be impressed to meet someone smart enough to want to know what's going on. If you damage your rapport with the very reasonable questions which follow and even lose the offer, I suggest that the place was no good to begin with and you've lost nothing, and perhaps have even been delivered from making a bad mistake.

Assuming you get your meeting with the senior decision maker for the company at whatever profit center level is appropriate, the most significant thing you want to gain is information about your proposed peers and those who may be superior to you but to whom you do not report. The questions are similar to those brought up previously—duration of employment with this firm, where they came from, personality types, management styles, attitudes toward business, perceived level of competence, and so forth.

It may be a good idea to get information about subordinates, particularly those who have been with the firm for ten years or more. If you are being offered responsibility for a large staff that includes some of these veterans, serious problems may quickly arise if you discover lack of performance on the part of even one of them. Many managers have taken new positions, evaluated such people in the course of their departmental overview, discovered what they perceive to be incompetence, and then have found to their horror that these people have an "in" at the very top and cannot be fired for any normal reason. Such people can quite literally make life hell for a manager evaluated on performance and, again, nobody will volunteer this kind of information; you must dig it out for yourself.

Another place where you may learn something useful is to find out about company projects and ventures. The person with whom you're speaking doubtless knows more than anyone below him about such things and should have a good idea of what is going on in other divisions of the company (if the company is a large one). A good question might be, "What is the most exciting thing happening around here these days?" Another might be, "What's the most important thing you're doing to improve profits this year?" Such questions can lead to interesting avenues of conversation and offer you real intelligence about the company at the same time.

Once you have received satisfactory answers to these types of questions, it remains only to verify the terms of your contract (if you have one) and you have a deal. Now comes the part about telling your current employers that you must leave their happy home. As we shall see, even that requires finesse.

15
Making a Clean Break

Offer in hand, secure in the knowledge that you want the position, you must now take the next step. If you are currently unemployed, this typically means skipping down to the local store for caviar and champagne to celebrate. Invite a few friends over to share your gladness at having found something good.

What, however, if you are still working? In this case you will take the earliest opportunity to go to your boss (who perhaps has been treating you like dirt for the last year) and cheerfully resign. If you're a talented person that the company doesn't want to lose, he or she will perhaps offer some muted congratulations and then begin to ask a few questions. Where are you going to work? How much are they offering you? What will your title be? Who will you report to? How many people will you be supervising? Then you may hear something like this:

"Gee, I'm sorry you're thinking of leaving us at this time. You've been slated for a raise of umpty-ump dollars which will go into effect next week. I just hadn't gotten around to telling you. Not only that, there's talk of making you a director and giving you responsibility over our other two departments here. We really don't want to lose you, and I think you've got a bright future here. Maybe you ought to reconsider."

This is called damage control. So many people fall for such blandishments that the subject cannot be glossed over. After all, if you've been with a firm for any length of time, even though things have been rough and you've felt unappreciated of late, there's a strong tendency to go with the devil you know rather the one you don't know. In the face of such generosity on the part of your boss, you may be tempted to stay. Perhaps you're thinking things have just been hectic and you haven't really been ignored. Perhaps getting passed over for promotion was some kind of oversight. Perhaps it will be possible to kiss and make up.

Forget it! Don't even consider it. Let the thought pass from your mind as quickly as it comes. You are being subjected to damage control maneuvers, and when you think about these things, remember the china plate. You can drop fine china on the floor and watch it break in five pieces. You can get out your epoxy glue, refit the pieces back together, wash it up and even eat from it, but it will never be the same. So it is with business marriages where divorce is threatened. By going to your employer and informing him that you intend to resign, you have committed treason. You are leaving the fold, deserting the family, departing from all that is good and pure, and, if you are going to work for a competitor, joining the opposing army as well. Regardless of the pleasant face that is put upon it, when a talented employee leaves a company, in their heart of hearts top management thinks of it as betrayal. Some companies believe this so deeply that if a person is found to be interviewing with other companies, he or she can be summarily fired and often are just for thinking about leaving. There are one or two limited cases in which you might consider remaining. Ninety-nine percent of the time, you should not.

Consider your boss's position. Your desk will be empty; work will pile up. There may not be anyone else inside the firm who can readily replace you. This means "you know who" gets to do your work. He will have to run ads and interview people on an emergency basis, attempting to get someone to fill your shoes as quickly as possible. Even if you give the standard two-week notice, the likelihood that you can be replaced in that period of time with a desirable new face is not high. Your departure may cause morale problems. If you are considered something of a leader in the office, others may decide to go also. All this runs through the boss's mind while he contemplates your leavetaking.

But there is a solution, at least from the boss's point of view. It may be crude, nasty, and highly unethical into the bargain, but it is a solution nonetheless and essentially costs the company nothing but its integrity, and that loss will not be widely broadcast. Betraying an employee has far fewer negative PR consequences than failing to honor one's guarantee, for example. The solution is simple: Entice the potential defectee with whatever inducements will make him or her stay, wait a few months to ensure that the opportunity for which the person was about to leave is no longer available, and then look for a replacement. A little blind box advertising, or a highly confidental third-party recruiter is the way to go. The boss can interview in the evening or during lunch hour outside the office and, when the ideal person is found, that individual who had threatened to resign can be quietly fired and the replacement brought aboard with little fuss. It is the perfect solution from the company's perspective.

Although a great deal of litigation concerns disgruntled employees suing former employers, most such suits are brought when the employers do something egregiously stupid, like telling them to their faces what they think of them. In the case I describe, if the firm handles its dirty business with care, and mumbles the usual garbage about changes in corporate policy, or a new organizational direction, the sad employee is left on the street without any understanding of what has happened. How can he sue? Upon what grounds? Even if he thinks he's been had, there is no way to prove it, unless confidential memos fall into his hands or he does an extraordinary amount of detective work to piece together the events which followed withdrawing his resignation and subsequent dismissal.

This is a nasty game, but you have to know that it's played frequently. The company may even be so bold as to organizationally eliminate the position, along with your employment and two months later reauthorize the position and bring into it the individual they have already identified. As I say, the cost to them is virtually nothing. The cost to you, if you are so unfortunate as to fall for their ploy, is astounding. You will have lost the opportunity you might have had and you will also be unemployed, which will seriously affect your ability to negotiate salary with your next employer.

Thus when the pie in the sky is materializing before your eyes in the words of your boss, who is so incredulous that you could be leaving at such a moment of great opportunity for you, remember that what the firm hath given the firm can take away. Please heed my advice, gained over years of listening to these sad tales of woe, and if you have decided to resign, *resign*. Think of all the reasons why you wanted to get out before this new development came up. Those things are real; you've lived with them every day. Contrast these realities with promises made by a person who has every motive in the world to make them and nothing that can compel him to keep them.

A variation on this theme is the "I need you" gambit. This may indeed be the case. The boss may have just lost a key employee and is now facing the loss of you. To further complicate matters, your boss may be an excellent human being, who has been fair and honorable with you at all times, and the principal difficulty is not him or her, but the company. Here, your sense of loyalty may be sorely tried, and you may decide "I've got to stick it out for Fran's sake." Pitfalls abound.

Fran may be looking. She may be as fed up with the place as you are. You don't know that, because Fran is probably too smart to advertise the fact. What happens if she leaves, Joe comes aboard, and you and Joe don't get along? Again, you have lost the opportunity, the job you decided to accept has been filled, and you are now in a far worse position than before.

A simple illustration may help, drawn from my own career in corporate life. As a department head for a reasonably large organization, where the crookedness of the owner was only exceeded by the incompetence of most of his senior staff, I had had enough after about a year. This considerably saddened an honorable, decent, and highly competent boss with whom I had worked closely. He understood, however, and wished me well. A few weeks afterward, I was called at my new job by one of my senior subordinates, who told me of an offer he had received—an excellent job with a good salary increase. "With you gone, now if I leave, he'll really be in the soup." I said that was true, but he'd best look out for his own interests since there was no likelihood the company would improve. We discussed it for a while, Paul thanked me and hung up.

Here is what actually happened. Paul decided to stay, turning down the very fine offer he had received. Meanwhile, unbeknownst to him, the boss, Mike, was at the same time interviewing for another position in a different state, entirely on the Q.T. Not two weeks after my friend Paul made his decision to remain with the company, Mike handed in his resignation and left. His replacement was of the same ethnic background as the owner and determined that nobody who didn't share that background was going to work for him. Paul was fired on the spot. So two weeks after making his decision to remain for Mike's benefit, Paul was on the street rather than sitting in his new office where he should have been. Readers take note; this could happen to you.

There is only one rule of thumb in these matters, it can be succinctly stated as follows: *Look out for Number One.* There is no room in this high-stakes contest for charity, altruism, compassion, or anything else. Nothing in all my years as a recruiter has ever led me to believe that companies will hesitate for one second to fire someone who has not been with them for a long time if they think efficiency or performance will be improved by that act. The people whom you work for will, if you are slated for dismassal, say all manner of things that are not true prior to the ax falling, if they deem it in their best interest to do so. Many hiring managers will work with a recruiter to find subordinates and, at the same time, be registered with that recruiter for placement elsewhere. At ten o'clock in the morning they are extolling the benefits of their company to the skies before an enraptured job candidate. At two that afternoon, they are on the phone to the recruiter who presented him, saying, "Get me out of here, I can't stand it anymore!" This kind of duplicity is standard in business, and it's not likely to change. The only way for you to protect yourself is insure that nothing deters you from the course that is in your own best interest based on known facts. Obviously, known facts do not include promises made by a boss who is desperate to keep you so that his department will run smoothly until such time as he can fire you on his own terms.

It may not be, however, that you are desperately seeking to leave your current employer but that you are exploring other opportunites and have found a very attractive one. Nevertheless, if your existing company could be persuaded to do a bit better for you, you would just as gladly stay as go. Many individuals in this situation will use the tactic of going to their current boss and saying, "I have such and such an offer from XYZ company and unless you match it or do better, I will leave." This is, quite frankly, the most foolish thing you can do, because it plays right into the hands of a person inclined to use damage control tactics. He will look at you aghast, offer a matching salary and perhaps a promotion, and you think you have won. What you don't know is that that afternoon he is devising plans to get rid of you on his own timetable.

Even when such situations do not result in immediate betrayal, the fact is that resignation, once threatened or carried out and then retracted, is remembered forever. When the economy turns bad, the person who has treated his or her employer with such disdain is likely to get the boot first. When promotions are being considered, that individual will have an extremely large black mark against his record. The long-term effects in the negative far outweigh the short-term benefits of using a new offer as a sword to hang over your employer's head for the purpose of extracting favors from him.

It is, however, not impossible to make use of your newly received offer while remaining with your current employer. The key is the attitude with which you approach your boss. I stress the importance of informality in many of these dealings because, if you don't let anyone know the gravity of a situation, he or she is much more likely to respond candidly than in a calculating manner.

Thus, offer in your pocket or purse, known only to you, you might approach your boss after work some evening and say something like, "you know, Bob, I've been here three years and have really enjoyed working with you. But it's been a while since my last raise, and I know the economy hasn't been good to us of late—what do you think my long-term prospects are?"

Bob may be the open and honest sort and respond, "Janet, I really don't know. I was in a board meeting last week and there's even talk of a hiring freeze. It could be two or three years before our department starts to expand again, but of course at that time you'd be the first one I'd pick for a vice-president."

How nice. An honest reply that indicates a two-year wait for promotion and, if a hiring freeze is contemplated, can a wage freeze be far behind? So you might respond, "Gee, I had no idea it was that bad. What are you going to do?"

If Bob is feeling convivial after a few snorts of the scotch he keeps in the bottom left-hand drawer, you might hear this eye-opening advice, "You ought to start looking around, because that's what I'm doing." This is intelligence of a high order and will help you make up your mind in a hurry. Of course, it's always possible that he may begin to sense the drift of the conversation and put on his PR hat for the company, assuring you that there may be clouds but the future is bright. . .blather, blather. A wise move at this point would be to pass the time of day for a few minutes, bid him a pleasant good evening, rush home and accept the offer.

If you have a genuinely Machiavellian boss, to whom even this casual discussion signals a potential desertion, he will perhaps begin the damage control process immediately. But now he has a problem—he doesn't know what your real plans are, and you will not confide in him if you have any sense. Therefore, if he offers you a raise and promotion at this point, it will have to be because you deserve it and the idea has already been in the works. He can't very well go to his own boss and say, "I gave the store away to Janet last night because we had a discussion about her career." With nothing more than that for evidence of possible defection, El Bosso may find himself on the street at that point. Companies don't appreciate their senior staff upsetting the applecart like that unless there is powerful justification for it. A friendly chat after work hardly qualifies as a smoking gun.

Therefore he will have to hedge, using such finely honed phrases as "We've got our eye on you" or "Your future is really bright with this company" or "There are a lot of changes going on right now that I can't talk about, but we know about your contributions to the firm and won't forget it."

This is all eyewash, of course. If the discssion about your career doesn't produce something concrete, it's because there isn't anything. If top management is genuinely considering you for betterment, your calculating boss will give you enough information to let you know he's not kidding, secure in the knowledge that top management will back him up if it gets to that. If nobody at the top has thought about you in the last two years, he will be reduced to offering boilerplate, and your tactic is the same: a pleasant good evening, the joyous phone call, and off to your new life.

There are some few instances where you can resign, be lured back, and not be seriously damaged. These typically occur in the sales and marketing fields, where your ability to produce is so valuable to the company that they will do almost anything to keep you and never dream of getting even because of that contribution. In such cases the blunt "I quit" may do you more good than any of the beating about the bush previously outlined. In other cases, if you are enticed back by promises of extraordinary reward, you might require that those promises be documented in the form of a very detailed contract. My rather cynical view of this business is that any promise made under damage control conditions can only be trusted to the extent that the company may be in for serious financial damage if the promises are broken. The only thing that will give that kind of leverage is a contract. Don't trust yourself with it; show it to a lawyer. Again, if the company doesn't want to do that, reaffirm your resignation and head for the greener pastures.

I don't mean to imply that every company is as cold and merciless as the situations I've been portraying would suggest. Some will indeed respond honorably to a threatened resignation by a valuable employee and offer promotions and increases, while treating that individual fairly throughout the rest of his or her career with that firm. Again, it is typically larger, better-known companies that react in mature fashion and play the game by civilized rules. My point remains, however, that in the absence of considerable historical evidence that your employer will act this way, you must never assume it. If you assume trickery and deceit, but don't let anybody know that's what you're thinking, and discover forthrightness and generosity, you will be quite pleasantly surprised. If you assume generosity and forthrightness, retract your resignation, and three months later discover trickery and deceit, you will be fired. The risk attached to the former tactic is small, while that of taking the more humanitarian view is far greater.

Let us assume that your mind is made up and the company cannot entice you back. You may be asked to go through an exit interview, so the company can learn some candid things about what you thought of your tenure with them, what you thought of management, and things of that nature.

This, too, is typically a feature of larger, more highly structured organizations, and I venture to say the great majority of businesses in this country don't bother with it. The smaller ones just wish you happy landings and that's that. But if you're asked to undergo an exit interview, you can't very well refuse without seeming churlish. Besides, you might want to get a few things off your chest.

This is precisely the wrong attitude to take. When you submit to this kind of interview, you should be on guard as at other times. Remember that, in this encounter, there may be a level of well-disguised or ill-disguised hostility because you have elected to leave the fold. The contents of the interview will be written and placed in your personnel jacket, so the wise course is caution, not frankness.

Resist the temptation to inform the exit interviewer that the reason you're leaving is that your boss is a woman-chasing lush. This may indeed be true, but consider the ramifications. Your boss may be advised of what was said about him (strictly in private, of course), but it's unlikely the company will take any drastic action unless these peculiarities of character begin to affect his work. He will, however, remember you and that comment and you may get less than a joyous reaction when, three years hence, he's asked for a reference on you. Just because you don't give his name in your list of references doesn't mean he won't be called, particulary if a diligent third-party recruiter is doing the checking. Remember too, that a clever person can sandbag a reference without saying anything that could be considered remotely libelous. True, the law has recently become so arcane that even silence has become grounds for litigation against a former employer, but why let yourself in for so much difficulty?

Your boss was wonderful, your company was wonderful, your job was wonderful; it's just that the situation to which you are going is more wonderful. Is it honest? Not really. But it is safe, and please be reminded that you have nothing to gain by answering with your true opinions, and a great deal to lose.

The corollary is that it is not dishonest, nor is your motive in making positive comments to harm anyone or deceive anyone in a material sense. I like to think of myself as someone with a reputation for integrity, but I will not hesitate to instruct people in exit interviews to be bland, cheerful, and generally positive about everything they say. Anyone who describes that sort of conduct as deception is asking for a level of purity that I suggest they themselves could not attain.

One other point, and we are through. In the exit interview you may be asked where you are going, what kind of job it is, how much you will be paid, and how you got the job in the first place. If any of these questions are asked, my advice is that you respond, "I really don't think it's necessary for us to go into that" or words to that effect. Your exit interviewer may get miffed and try to press, but you should respond with the same sentiment couched in different words. There is a reason for this.

As the great industrialist said, who was found driving drunk in a strange city in the company of a woman who was not his wife, upon being promptly thrown in jail, "Never complain, never explain."

If you tell them where you're going, it opens the door for them to disparage your new company. If you agree with them, you sound like a fool, if you defend the new firm, it could conceivably turn into a shouting match. Likewise, if you tell them how much you'll be making or what kind of job you've been offered, you may be chided for selling yourself short or not doing as well as you could have if you'd stayed where you were. Again, a confrontation may result. And if you tell them how you found the job, it may give them opportunites to cast aspersions on your loyalties once more.

What I'm saying is this: If you answer questions like these, you leave yourself open to cross-examination. Cross-examination can turn to conflict, conflict can turn to argument, and argument can turn to shouting. Your exit interview will be a fiasco, your personnel jacket may contain some very choice comments on your "immaturity" written by the person with whom you had disagreement, and who knows what may result years hence as you try to build your career.

Conversely, you may answer all those questions frankly and truthfully, and be thanked for your candor and bid a fond farewell. What has it gained you? I can virtually guarantee you that nothing will go into your personnel jacket about how pleasantly you handled the exit interview; it's not important to the company. Thus the situation produces the possibility of high risk and virtually zero gain. I think it is better to use the silent approach and avoid potential conflict altogether. If you are pleasant but firm in your refusal to discuss such things, there is very little the exit interviewer can do.

It's the corporate equivalent of taking the Fifth Amendment at a Senate committee organized-crime hearing. If the mobster sticks to the same old phrase, scripted by his lawyer, he's fine. If, on the other hand, he starts to answer questions, he's fair game and may wind up in jail. Why take the risk? We are not mobsters, but the principle is sound.

To you I say, go and do likewise. The company will not resent you for being firm, and you will leave under the best possible circumstances.

16
Heading Out onto the Field

We have come to the end. Ideally, if you follow every instruction in this book exactly as presented, you should come up with several offers for excellent positions at outstanding companies. Unfortunately, this is not an ideal world, and it doesn't always work that way.

You have to take an objective view of the whole hiring situation, which is admittedly rather difficult, since you will clearly be emotionally wrapped up in your own career and your own future. Nevertheless, you will collect a certain number of "rejection slips" in the process of moving from one job to another over the course of your career, and the only way to keep yourself stable when they arrive at your door is to look at things for what they are, not what they seem to be.

As you've seen by now, I hope, the process by which many companies arrive at their determination of what is needed in a job candidate is by no means scientific. On countless occasions we have known of openings in the business community where, when all was said and done, the candidate selected bore not even a passing resemblance to the original specifications. The emotional nature of the decision makes deviation from written standards easy, particularly when one person can make the decision autonomously. If the warm fuzzy orange ball rises up in him or her, it is not uncommon for that and that alone to be the deciding factor. As bizarre as the idea may have sounded to you at first, let me assure you that if your competitor for a professional position has produced that feeling in the hiring manager, it is virtually certain he will get an offer. That's not something you can control—don't worry about it.

The fact is, you will not get along with everybody. Some people will like your style; others will not. Some people will come away from an interview with you having a certain impression about you; others will come away with an exactly opposite view. This is not a reflection on you, but on them. You cannot really change what you have become over the course of your working life and, aside from the slight modifications required for a good presentation, which we have already gone through, the company has to take you pretty much as you are. Except in the case of trainees, few firms are so foolish as to hire people in positions of responsibility and then train them out of their bad habits.

In many cases, your background simply will not fit the company's legitimate requirements. That may not have been obvious to anybody at the outset, including you, but if the company has done a credible job of evaluation they will learn that your talents and abilities are not well suited to their needs. They will let you know, briefly and politely, and this is no defeat for you. Again, you are what you are, and there is no profit in self-flagellation about what you might have done to get the job. The fact is that, had you been hired, you might have found yourself on the street three months later when what should have been discovered in the interview process was discovered on the firing line; namely, that you weren't cut out for the job.

Finally, as happens all too often, your interviewer may just not be capable enough to discern the value you could bring to his organization. Ineffective interviewers are numerous, particularly among line managers, and, notwithstanding your diligent efforts to get certain information through, it may simply not be enough and another person may be chosen, even though you could have done a magnificent job. Again, there is nothing you can do but make the best possible presentation and hope that the other factors are in your favor.

The truth is that you can't really "make them choose you." I probably should have titled the book *Help Them Choose You,* but that's not as catchy. "Make" is a word that implies coercion, and you obviously can't force anybody to hire you unless you "have something" on them, at which point your interviewing talents are of less interest than that picture you're carrying around in your wallet. A peculiar way to get work, but I've seen *that* one, too.

Nevertheless, what I've tried to show in these pages is that you can indeed "help" the company make a decision in your favor. You can indeed motivate them to choose you over other competitors for the same position by a combination of presentation and tactical responses that cause you to appear to be the most attractive candidate they can find. If, before reading this, you have felt something like a pawn in a game you didn't understand when going on a job interview, I trust you now feel a bit more well armed for the contest. In fact, there are no mysteries to the interview ritual. There are only understandable agenda and processes which, because they are completely hidden from the job applicant, seem irrational and confusing at times. If this peek behind the scenes has helped you to make more sense of it, well and good.

Don't try to be something you're not; be the best you can

be. Remember that no matter how talented you really are, you must *appear* talented to merit further consideration by the company. Keep in mind the extraordinary limitations the interviewer must deal with in attempting to learn what you yourself know perfectly well—the extent and depth and configuration of your experiences and abilities. The interviewer will make a decision based upon what *he* knows about you, not upon what you know about you.

Help them choose you, persuade them to choose you, motivate them to choose you, encourage them to choose you, and you will have done all that can be done.

In negotiation, consider the relative desperation levels—yours and the company's. How empty is your refrigerator? How unique is your talent? How badly do they need someone and how long have they been looking? Bargain accordingly.

Don't be afraid to get tough once the firm throws the switch and actually offers you the job. You'll recall that in the initial stages the hiring manager wants to solve a problem for which you are being evaluated as a possible element in the solution. Now, if you will follow me, once the company has made the offer, the hiring manager is attempting to solve another problem, namely getting you to take the job. That shift in focus once the offer is made will allow you to bargain fairly hard in some cases, provided you remain pleasant, diplomatic, and appropriately deferential throughout the negotiation.

In these delicate situations, even though you think you've got the upper hand, courtesy costs nothing and pays great dividends. Remember, it remains an emotional experience for the manager until the deal is done, and he always has the option, if you should choose to come on snooty, to shut down the whole thing for his ego's sake. I've seen it happen, so just keep in mind that the game is played in the company's ball park, with the company's ball and by the company's rules.

When you land a good offer with a good company and you're currently employed in a situation that isn't desperate, don't give the new folks an answer right away. Ask for a few days to think about it; after all, it's a major decision and they shouldn't begrudge you some time to mull it over so long as you don't ask them to wait too long—a few days for lower-level jobs, rarely more than two weeks unless the position is well into six figures, and then it can be months.

Go back to your current boss and, without letting him know what's afoot, find out whether there are any attractive plans for you that haven't yet been disclosed. You may discover a big promotion in the works, in which case you may want to think twice about taking the new job. Better the devil you know . . . But, as is usually the case when the boss has no ulterior motive to make things appear rosier than they are, you may find out that nothing is scheduled to change for months, or even years. This in itself is reinforcement, something to make you feel good about moving on.

Good hunting, my friend. Changing jobs is a tough, sometimes dirty business but, if you're any kind of professional at all, you will probably have to do it several times in your working life. You may as well know how to do it right. In these circumstances, altruism, loyalty, and other more noble aspects of human nature simply have no place. You have to look out for Number One because, almost invariably, companies will not look out for you. There are myriads of horror stories about people who failed to recognize this essential fact and suffered badly for it. Keep that in mind while you play the game.

There are some very good jobs out there and, as the saying goes, plenty of room at the top for responsible, diligent, competent people. But to prove you are all those things, you must first get the opportunity.

My purpose has been to make your opportunities more numerous and your choices more certain. It is my hope that these ideas may help steer you through a successful and rewarding career.